MARTIAL ARTS
AFTER 40

MARTIAL ARTS
AFTER 40

by
Sang H. Kim Ph.D.

Turtle Press   **Hartford**

MARTIAL ARTS AFTER 40

Exercise Photographs by Marc Yves Regis

To contact the author or to order additional copies of this book:
Turtle Press
401 Silas Deane Hwy
P.O. Box 290206
Wethersfield, CT 06129-0206
1-880-77-TURTL

ISBN 1-880336-29-4
LCCN 99-44144
Printed in the United States of America

Library of Congress Cataloguing in Publication Data

Kim, Sang H.
Martial arts after 40 / by Sang H. Kim.
p.   cm.
Includes index.
ISBN 1-880336-29-4
1. Martial arts. I. Title. II. Title: Martial arts after forty
GV1101.K54
796.8--dc21   99-44144

Contents

MARTIAL ARTS
AFTER 40

"Aren't you too old for martial arts?"

Have you heard this question lately? Or perhaps even looked in the mirror and asked yourself the same thing? Well the answer is a resounding "No." Martial arts can be practiced as long as, if not longer, than just about any other physical pursuit.

In fact, martial artists often get better, not worse, with age. Perhaps you are not as fast or flexible as the younger students in class. Perhaps you don't recover as quickly from your workouts or you are bothered by new aches and pains that you easily shook off when you were younger. These are minor obstacles when you consider the benefits that come with age. The wisdom to slow down, to see the lessons in every class, to mentor younger students, to laugh at the macho posturing and go your own way, to discover yourself from the inside out. That is what martial arts after 40 is about; a journey of self, a discovery of the boundlessness of your mind and body, working as one, expressing your inner joy and wisdom.

Aging is an inevitable process. It proceeds at different rates in different people. You can't stop it, but you can delay it. It is your responsibility to live your life to the fullest - or not. As your life unfolds, you begin to realize that every choice that you have made so far has brought definite consequences that are either rewarding or painful. Reaching mid-life means an accumulation of wisdom. Based upon the lessons of your past choices, you now have a great opportunity to reconsider and possibly change the course of your life. In fact, now is the perfect time to begin living your life to the fullest.

The very fact that you are a martial artist or are considering taking up the martial arts means you want to take care of yourself, that you want to challenge your mind and body. This choice is a tremendous gift to yourself. It means that you can reach the point of being where your body and mind coexist in perfect harmony.

In your martial arts training, you will at some point realize that your body is unique in itself. Your body has a different set-point from others. You have to learn to adjust your condition to the ideal point for the uniqueness of your body. You can ignore statistics and standard guidelines, but you cannot take your natural guidelines for granted.

This book is not intended to mold you to be like someone you see on the cover of a fitness magazine. Instead, it will help you realistically get into and stay in the physical condition that will allow you to continue to enjoy your martial arts practice for many years to come.

Book I

BEGINNING YOUR JOURNEY

chapter 1

Healthy Body
Healthy Mind

Before we begin looking at how to get and stay fit for martial arts, let's take a look at why fitness is increasingly important when we grow older. As we grow older, our habits often change. We spend more time at work and less time at play. This trend can lead to an increasingly sedentary life-style. The more sedentary you become, the less energy you can generate. Less energy means the loss of efficiency in your biological systems. Over the years, the more inefficient you become, the more demands your body places on itself, leading to a downward spiral of deteriorating health.

But this does not have to be the case. You can keep your body functioning properly through good nutrition, good sleeping habits and regular exercise. You gain energy through sensible eating habits, expand your energy through physical activity, and restore your energy during resting periods. When you eat sensibly you feel energetic. When you increase your activity level, your metabolism increases, burning more calories from food eaten and fat stored. In fact, an active metabolism continues to burn calories even while resting, if you consistently work out. In addition to an enhanced metabolism, regular exercise lowers your blood pressure, slows your respiratory rate, improves your mood, relieves insomnia, enhances your flexibility and strength, and increases the flow of oxygen throughout your body. With all of these benefits, you can't afford not to exercise.

FITNESS IS NATURAL

Being fit is natural: The human body is built for movement. It is a biomechanical device made to move. So when it stops moving, it deteriorates. In terms of physical fitness, mid-life is an important stage of life that provides an opportunity to look back and forward. It is a time of realization that, after running the race for four decades, aging is inevitable and you are not going to get any younger. Ongoing deterioration of the body begins to take place.

Movement is like medicine as the body ages. It is the only unifying bond between your body and your mind. It creates changes in your personality. Until you start to move your body in new ways, such as those in martial arts, you don't know very much about your body. When you begin to move, it reveals the weaknesses of your body. It creates an urgency within you to do something about them.

Since life is movement and movement is life, the more you move the more you desire to live. Movement is the central secret to a fulfilling life experience. More movement means more life. Less movement means diminished life. The secret is simple. Be more active. You don't have to be a great athlete. Enjoy your martial arts training and other physical pursuits. By focusing on the enjoyment of the movements rather than competition or strict goals, you can maintain a positive attitude and stay motivated.

Ideally, to keep your body in shape for martial arts, you should do thirty to sixty minutes of moderate physical activity every day. Include a variety of activities in your routine such as stretching exercises, aerobic activity, and light strength training. If you are just beginning, build your routine progressively. Don't do too much at once. And remember to always warm up before training and cool down after exercise. Warming up is more necessary than ever in avoiding injuries as your body ages. Most importantly, be consistent in rewarding yourself for what you have accomplished.

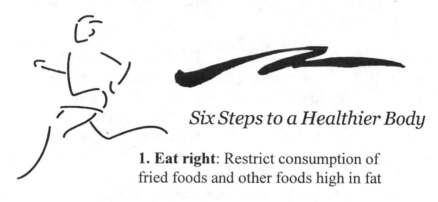

Six Steps to a Healthier Body

1. Eat right: Restrict consumption of fried foods and other foods high in fat

2. Be active: Exercise lowers the blood pressure.

3. Develop healthy habits: Drink more water, limit alcohol consumption, don't smoke or use tobacco.

4. Maintain optimal weight: Eat sensibly and burn what you eat every day.

5. Release stress: Engage in hobbies that involve mind and body activities.

6. Think young: Cultivate the right attitude toward aging.

HEALTHY BODY

The concept of fitness has significantly changed over the past decade. The most important reason for exercising in this decade is to feel right about yourself by having a sense of improved health. The second most important reason is the desire to feel better and live longer. The benefits traditionally associated with being fit—looking better and losing weight—are not as important to those over the age of 40. Only one-fifth of adults over 40 think losing weight is important, and only ten percent report improved appearance as a top reason for exercising.

Surprisingly more than half of people over 40 still believe that it's necessary to work out intensely a minimum of thirty minutes at a time to get the full benefits of exercise. In contrast, the most recent discoveries recommend that even moderate activity in short spurts can improve overall health and increase longevity. According to the American College of Sports Medicine and the President's Council on Physical Fitness and Sports, moderate physical activity can impart many of the long-term health benefits associated with more intense workouts.

The most common barrier to the exercise, according to the joint studies, is identified as lack of motivation. Half of the respondents say they can't motivate themselves to start exercising; one-fourth say they fear they won't be able to keep up with a fitness program; and one-fifth say they just don't know how to get started.

Most people over 40 (78 percent) believe that launching an exercise regimen becomes more and more difficult with advancing age. In reality though, you need to exercise your body to prevent early deterioration. Reasonable levels of daily activity are a vital part of growing older. The key is to lead a more active life-style in general. Through a dynamic life style, you can easily develop the habit of exercise.

Activities such as brisk walking, hiking, stair-climbing, aerobic exercise, calisthenics, resistance training, jogging, running, bicycling, rowing, swimming, and sports such as tennis, racquetball, soccer, basketball, and martial arts are especially beneficial when performed regularly.

The training effect of such activities is most apparent at exercise intensities exceeding 40% to 50% of exercise capacity. (Exercise capacity is defined as the point of maximum ventilator oxygen uptake or the highest work intensity that can be achieved.) Evidence also supports that even low- to moderate-intensity activities performed daily can have some long-term health benefits and lower the risk of cardiovascular disease. Low-intensity activities include walking for pleasure, gardening, yard work, house work, dancing, and prescribed home exercise.

Keys to fitness after 40:

After 40
Fitness
Tip

1) Positive Attitude
   - Treat your body properly
   - Have a positive attitude
   - Have a flexible approach
   - Think young
2) Exercise
3) Nutrition

Longevity:
Empower Your Life Style

Life-style affects your life span. Those who live healthy, stay youthful and get happier as they get older. They have a more assertive and positive mental disposition. The following are some observations of the characteristics of those who live to be 90 or more:

1) They live an unhurried pace of life.
2) They are optimistic and positive thinkers.
3) They stay close to nature.
4) They drink sufficient water daily.
5) They are active.
6) They have very moderate eating habits.
7) They have meaningful pursuits throughout their lives.
8) They avoid distress-fear, anxiety, depression, alienation.
9) They enjoy physical challenges and excitement.
10) They have valuable support.
11) They are honest.
12) They foster honest relationships.
13) They stay interested in life.
14) They choose their own course.
15) They are givers.
16) They respond creatively to changes.
17) They have high levels of adaptability and flexibility.
18) They feel comfortable with themselves.
19) They enjoy time alone rather than see it as loneliness.
20) They appreciate their uniqueness.

Develop these qualities in yourself by:

- Identifying your weaknesses/shortcomings.
- Practicing perceiving situations positively.
- Viewing problems as challenges rather than obstacles.
- Starting or maintaining a fitness program.
- Developing coping skills.
- Determining your priorities.
- Learning how to adapt.
- Welcoming changes rather than resisting them.
- Taking breaks regularly.
- Avoiding judgments.
- Cultivating healthy relationships.
- Setting a variety of short-term goals.
- Being a good family member.
- Taking it easy.
- Spending time outdoors/enjoying nature.
- Practicing being alone without feeling lonely.
- Sharing your time or talents with others.
- Celebrating your individuality.
- Pursuing creative opportunities.

HEALTHY MIND

Regular exercise helps you concentrate better and improves your mood. With a million things going on in your mind, you cannot have the focus to solve one problem well. Exercise shifts your mind from inside-you to outside-you. It distracts you from the problems and thoughts cluttering your mind. When your mind is clear, you can be more effective and creative. Your mood will be significantly elevated after a thirty to forty-five minute workout. The change reportedly results from the increased circulation of the brain chemicals: catecholamines and endorphins.

Catecholamines are adrenaline related compounds in the brain that are known to elevate the mood. Exercise increases the level of catecholamines in the brain, thereby improving your mood. Endorphins are drugs the body produces to make pain tolerable. Exercise is a strenuous process of breaking down cells in the body. Since your brain translates the process as a series of injuries, the body triggers the brain to release endorphins to cover the discomfort. This release brings you a form of euphoria that elevates your mood.

A person in healthy physical and mental condition is better able to take in charge of his or her own life, personally and professionally. Whereas a person who is chronically tired and depressed is more likely to be controlled by circumstances than to take control of his or her own life.

Slow down the aging process in your everyday life by taking the following actions daily:

» Accept your aging

» Adjust your expectations

» Cope with changes

» Ask why

» Have a sense of purpose

» Be willing

» Change your environment

» Take action

» Take responsibility

» Approach things with a positive attitude

» Fill every day with dreams

» Treasure your achievement

» Let it go

COUNTER-AGING

FITNESS BENEFITS AFTER 40

Age 40 is the beginning of a new life. It is the starting point for maintaining good health. An appropriate regular exercise program can help you achieve this goal. Many of the physiologic changes that occur with aging were formerly thought to be due to the aging process itself. However, routine exercise is now known to have the following benefits that counteract the aging process:

- Reduces the risk of heart disease by improving blood circulation throughout the body.

- Keeps weight under control.

- Improves blood cholesterol levels.

- Prevents and manages high blood pressure.

- Prevents bone loss.

- Boosts energy levels.

- Helps you manage stress.

- Releases tension.

- Improves the ability to fall asleep quickly and sleep well: A Stanford School of Medicine study shows that thirty to forty minute exercise sessions four times a week can result in an extra hour of sleep a night and reduce the time it takes to fall asleep by half.

- Improves self-image and self-esteem.

- Counters anxiety and depression. Increases enthusiasm and optimism.

- Increases muscle strength, giving greater capacity for other physical activities.

- Provides a way to share an activity with family and friends. (Especially martial arts!)

- Helps delay or prevent chronic illnesses and diseases associated with aging and maintains quality of life and independence longer.

- Slows down physiologic decline.

- Reduces the desire to smoke.

- Prevents chronic and degenerative conditions.

- Prevents diabetes: Exercise increases the sensitivity to insulin, induces weight loss, and improves glucose tolerance. Moderate physical activity may prevent non-insulin dependent diabetes, especially in those at high risk due to body weight, history of hypertension, or a parental history of diabetes.

- Prevents osteoarthritis, osteoporosis and arteriosclerosis.

- Improves balance and coordination, which can reduce the likelihood of falling related injuries.

Most people over forty today are younger in many ways than their parents were when they were the same age. Physical fitness and nutritional awareness have brought significant advancements in health care. People are living longer and enjoying it more. In addition to the many physical benefits listed above, exercise also improves one's general sense of well being and outlook on life. A well-rounded fitness program can slow and even reverse many of the factors associated with aging.

THINKING POINTS

1. Fitness after 40 for martial arts training entails a daily commitment of thirty to sixty minutes of moderate activity including walking, jogging, weight training, and/or aerobic activity.

2. Exercise has many benefits after age 40 including reducing depression and anxiety, controls weight, prevents high blood pressure, reduces stress, prevents chronic diseases, and slows the aging process.

3. Exercise reduces anxiety and depression by releasing mood elevating drugs into the blood stream.

4. Many seemingly age related problems can be minimized or eliminated with a regular exercise program.

chapter 2

The ABC's of Fitness

There are three elements for optimal physical fitness for adult men and women: cardiovascular fitness, muscular fitness and weight management.

1) Cardiovascular Fitness

Your heart is the most important muscle in your body. When it is working properly, your body's systems can function at peak efficiency. To keep your heart in good working order, you need to get regular aerobic exercise.

Moderate exercise of long duration (more than ten minutes) relies on the presence of oxygen for energy supplies and therefore creates a fairly consistent energy demand in the body. When oxygen is present during an activity, it is called **aerobic** exercise. Examples of aerobic exercise in the martial arts are prolonged drills, shadow sparring, fast paced forms practice and extended periods of heavy bag work.

When exercise takes place in the absence of oxygen, it is **anaerobic** activity. During anaerobic exercise, the energy for an activity is supplied directly from high-energy phosphate compounds stored in the muscles being used. Examples of anaerobic activities in the martial arts are short bursts of target kicking, self-defense practice and interval bag training. In these activities, when the duration is a few minutes or less, the method of energy production results in the production of the waste product lactic acid. Muscle pain often occurs after anaerobic exercise due to the accumulation of the waste product in the muscles.

Some exercises require a blend of aerobic and anaerobic energy production. Usually this type of exercise is characterized by bursts of intense exercise interspersed with longer periods of more moderate exercise. A good example of this is sparring in which periods of bouncing and moving around (aerobic) are interspersed with brief but intense flurries of kicks and punches (anaerobic).

It is important to mix anaerobic exercise with aerobic exercise. Many martial arts activities can be done aerobically or anaerobically depending on the format. For example, practicing a short form once at full power is anaerobic while practice a form ten times successively at moderate power is aerobic. Doing ten rapid kicks to the heavy bag and resting for a minute is anaerobic while working the bag moderately for three five minute rounds with a thirty second rest between rounds is aerobic.

2) Muscular Fitness

There are three types of muscular fitness: muscular strength, endurance and flexibility. Muscular strength and endurance are increased by the consistent process of breaking down and repairing muscle tissue. Exercise causes muscle tissue to burst and break. When rested and reconstructed, it gets stronger than before the breakdown. Adequate rest between workouts plays an important role in repairing the tissue. If you work very hard on improving your kicks on Monday, give your legs a rest on Tuesday so the muscles can recuperate.

Muscular flexibility is achieved through the regular use of the muscles through a full range of motion. Daily stretching will allow you to improve or maintain your flexibility for as long as you stay active in the martial arts. In addition to stretching, try to make use of your full range of motion when practicing kicks, strikes and throws.

3) Weight Management

The key to maintaining your weight lies in managing your metabolism. When your metabolism is elevated through physical training, it remains high even hours after training. That means more calories continue to be burned long after you finish your workout. (*See the weight management section in Chapter 3 for more details.*)

PACE YOURSELF

It is very important to pace your efforts when you exercise. The goal is not to tire too quickly, but to gain the benefits of being active. Pacing yourself is especially important if you have not been active before or if you are increasing your training intensity. For the first two weeks, aim at the lowest part of your target heart rate (50 percent). Then progressively build up to the higher zone of the target rate (75 percent). After six to seven months, you should be able to push yourself comfortably up to 85 percent of your maximum heart rate. But remember that you do not have to exercise that hard to stay in shape.

How to Raise your Heart Rate

After 40 Fitness Tip

1) Do exercises that are rhythmic.

2) Do exercises that are repetitive.

3) Do exercises that involve motion using large muscles.

4) Do exercises that challenge your circulatory system.

TARGET HEART RATE AFTER 40

Your target heart rate is 50 to 75 % of your maximum heart rate. You should measure your pulse periodically as you exercise and stay within your target range. There are two reasons why target heart rate is important to you: it tells you your initial fitness level and it allows you to monitor your progress after you begin exercising.

The alternative to the target heart rate is the "conversational pace" test. If you can talk and kick at the same time, you should be working harder.

The following are estimated target heart rates:

Age	Target Heart Rate	Maximum HR
40 years	90–135 beats per minute	180
45 years	88–131 beats per minute	175
50 years	85–127 beats per minute	170
55 years	83–123 beats per minute	165
60 years	80–120 beats per minute	160
65 years	78–116 beats per minute	155
70 years	75–113 beats per minute	150

How to measure your target heart rate: Subtract your age from 220 and multiply by .60 and .75. Example for a 40-year-old: 220-40=180. 180X.60=108 beats per minute. 180X.75=135 beats per minute. Thus, a 40-year-old's target health rate is between 108 and 135 beats per minute.

FITNESS CAUTIONS

If you have any of the following conditions, you are advised to see your doctor before you begin any serious training according to the American College of Sports Medicine.

- hypertension

- cholesterol greater than 240 mg/dl

- cigarette smoking

- diabetes

- family history of heart disease before age 55

- symptoms of cardiopulmonary or metabolic disease

- chest pain

- dizziness

- ankle swelling

- rapid heart rate (greater than 100 bpm)

- claudication (pain with movement of a limb)

- heart murmur

You should pay close attention to any of these signals and see a physician for guidelines.

Additionally, consider the following cautions before you begin a new exercise or training regimen:

1. Create a tailored exercise program with your physician's input.

2. If you have hypertension, avoid activities that cause prolonged breath holding, which tends to increase blood pressure. Also avoid choking techniques which might put pressure on the arteries in your neck and your windpipe.

3. If you are on medication, you may need an adjustment in your exercise program or medication.

4. If you have diabetes, glucose levels may need to be monitored closely because exercise and weight loss may reduce insulin requirements.

5. If you have had hip or knee surgery, you should avoid the following unless your doctor gives you the okay:

- Running

- Jogging

- Kicking

- Sparring

- Exercises that involve kneeling

6. Closely follow any other limitations your physician places on your exercise regimen.

EXERCISE PRINCIPLES

1) The Overload Principle

A well organized and effective training program takes into account frequency, intensity, and duration of training. To improve in any physical pursuit, you must increase one or more of these factors. By increasing the frequency, intensity or duration of an activity beyond what your body is normally capable of, you create a physiologic overload. Exercising any system in your body under overload conditions forces the system to adapt to a greater demand and increase it's ability to perform.

You can create overload effectively by increasing any of the three factors, however, you must make sure that the increase keeps pace with your body's ability to cope with the overload. If you are not creating enough overload, your body will maintain its gains, but further gains will be minimal. If you increase your training suddenly or drastically, you may get injured, preventing further progress.

Frequency: How many days per week?

Ideally you should exercise six days a week. This does not mean you have to practice martial arts every day. You can dedicate two or three days to martial arts practice and three or four days to another exercise activity like jogging, swimming, weight training, stretching, calisthenics, or bicycling. If you want to overload your frequency, you can do martial arts more frequently, even up to five days a week if you feel you won't get burned out. Obviously the potential to increase the frequency of your training is not infinite. At some point, other demands on your time will limit how much time you can dedicate to training and to fitness overall.

Intensity: How hard?

Alternate the intensity of your workouts, going hard one day and taking it easy the next day. You may also alternate working on upper body skills one day and lower body skills the next day if your practice level is very intense. Increasing the intensity of your workouts on your "hard" days is a great way to improve your martial arts conditioning and skills. A sample plan might include high intensity sparring, drilling and heavy bag workouts on Monday and Wednesday, a high intensity cardio workout on Friday and lighter sessions including stretching, forms practice and weapons work on Tuesday, Thursday, and Saturday.

Duration: Length of each session?

For best results, each workout should be at least 30 minutes in duration. Between thirty and sixty minutes is ideal. A shorter workout might focus on just one activity while a longer workout, such as a martial arts class might include a warm-up, stretching, martial arts skills practice, calisthenics and a cool down period. Like frequency, duration is not infinitely expandable. If you are short on time, work exercise into your daily routine like a brisk walk at lunch or a workout at the park while your kids play on the swings.

2) Specificity Principle

Since a specific category of exercise (such as cardiovascular or strength) generally has minimal effect on other systems of the body once you are in good fundamental shape, you should focus your training on activities that are directly related to your martial arts practice. As a rule, specific exercise elicits specific adaptations creating specific training results. This simply means that while lifting weights improves your overall strength capacity, it doesn't necessarily improve your punching power or skill. The best way to improve punching is to punch. In the same way, while running improves your endurance and leg strength, it doesn't necessarily improve your ability to have fresh legs after four or five sparring matches. The best way to improve your muscular and cardiovascular endurance for sparring is to spar regularly.

Cross training is great for improving your overall fitness level and maintaining your weight, but you should not expect it to take the place of martial arts practice. Balance your non-martial arts fitness activities with direct practice of the martial arts skills you need to improve.

3) Individuality Principle

The results you get from working out are contingent on your unique potential as an individual. If you attend a martial arts class, you may find that students are expected to learn a homogenized curriculum and perform to certain standards regardless of age or background. Depending on your instructor, there may be exceptions made for students who are too young, too old or have special physical limitations that prevent them from performing up to the group standards.

If you find that you are having difficulty with a particular part of the curriculum, talk to your instructor privately so he or she can help you devise a home training plan to supplement your in-class practice. As you grow older, you may find that you have to do extra work at home to keep up with the class, particularly in the areas of flexibility and advanced techniques. Don't get discouraged. Everyone improves at their own pace and it is unreasonable to expect every student to respond in the same way to a particular training program.

4) Reversibility Principle

The reversibility principle states that a certain level of training (overload) must be maintained to prevent deconditioning or loss of capacity. In fact, it is estimated that once a training program is discontinued, improvements made through training are lost in five to ten weeks. For this reason, it is important to start or return to training gradually. While you may already be a black belt, if you suffer an injury and lose six weeks of training, you should start back at white belt level for a few weeks until you regain your black belt level of conditioning.

Similarly, if you have not been training regularly (at least twice a week), you should not expect to go full force when you do attend class. While your mind may know the techniques, your body may not be willing or able to follow, resulting in a serious joint or muscle injury. Nothing is more important to injury prevention in the martial arts than working within your body's level of conditioning.

1. There are three elements of fitness: cardiovascular fitness, muscular fitness and weight management.

2. Cardiovascular exercise can be either aerobic (with oxygen) or anaerobic (without oxygen). Martial arts class is often a blend of aerobic and anaerobic training.

3. Muscular fitness includes muscle strength, flexibility, and muscle endurance.

4. The target (most beneficial) heart rate for aerobic exercise is 50 to 75% of your maximum heart rate.

5. Before beginning any exercise program, consult your physician and note any symptoms on the fitness cautions check list.

6. If you are on medication, you may need to adjust your exercise level, medication dosage or both.

7. To benefit from an exercise, it must create an overload on the system(s) you are targeting to improve. Overload can be created by increasing the intensity, frequency or duration of an activity.

8. Exercise is most beneficial when it is specific to the activity you want to improve.

9. Once a training program is discontinued, improvements made through training are lost in five to ten weeks. If you take time off from martial arts, start back at a lower level of intensity than you left off at.

Diet and Nutrition
for Martial Artists

The body is divided into two types of matter: mass and fat. Mass includes bone, muscle, vital organs, and fluid. Fat has two kinds: brown fat and white fat. Brown fat insulates your organs and helps the body function. The more the better. White fat is excess stored calories. It's function is to insulate the outer body and to provide energy when needed. Excess white fat stresses your heart and causes obesity. Fat deposits build up when you eat more calories than you burn. Any excessive intake of nutrients such as fat, protein or carbohydrates is stored in the form of white fat. This is what most people try to get rid of when they go on a diet.

THE PITFALLS OF DIETING

Dieting is a losing battle. Why? You will gain back the amount that you lost soon as you return to your regular eating habits. Dieting only serves to shock your body. The body works against shock. Therefore, diet is an unnatural act that triggers the built-in defense system in the body against unnatural acts.

Scientists call it hypocaloric suppression of the basic metabolic rate, which is a starvation defense system of the body. It's main function is for survival. When you don't eat, the suppression mechanism begins to work and your body slows down its metabolism. Your body, then, nourishes itself by burning body fat and protein from muscle tissue. This suppression allows you to survive on less food intake in desperate times, for example if you were stranded on a deserted island.

What happens when the diet ends? A rebound effect. The body absorbs nutrition like a sponge to refill the amount that was lost while dieting. The resumption of food immediately sets the mode of the body to initiate organic stores of nutrition to prepare for the next period of starvation. When the next diet begins, the body repeats the same cycle. Each time is a tremendous shock to the body's entire system.

Dieting reduces the number of calories you take in. Reducing the number of calories you take in does not create long-term weight loss unless you do it along with an exercise program designed to burn excess fat. One pound of body fat takes 3500 calories. If you cut 100 calories a day out of your diet, it takes 35 days to lose one pound. Although dieting accelerates weight loss, it does not necessarily mean losing excess fat. You may lose muscle which is denser and heavier than fat. So it is important that you burn fat by exercising while you reduce your calorie intake by permanently modifying your eating habits.

In fact, weight gain or loss is not the best measuring tool for the health of your body. If you begin exercising and change your eating habits, you might end up weighing more than you did when you began. If you build muscle, which is denser and heavier than fat, while losing excess fat, your body will be leaner and stronger but not necessarily lighter.

Be persistent and patient. It takes time to change your body's rhythm. Give your body time to adjust to what your mind has decided. Once you gain momentum, it is a lot easier. It might become a way of life. Stick with it!

BASIC FORMULA FOR WEIGHT CONTROL

Everyone has a different optimal physical condition. Your body has its own unique internal mechanism that constantly tends toward the weight and shape that is ideal for you. When you are sensible about your body, weight control is a natural process. It means that your body will gradually gravitate to the weight ideal for you.

Successful weight control doesn't mean you have to be thin. Rather, that you can reach and maintain your best weight.

There are two factors that are important for weight control: caloric intake and energy output. The ideal method for losing weight is to combine sensible eating and exercise.

Most women can lose an average of one to two pounds a week by consuming 1200-1500 calories a day. Most men can lose this amount by consuming 1500-1800 calories a day. One to two pounds a week is the ideal maximum rate of weight loss. The formula to find the daily amount of food intake are as follow:

> To maintain your body weight, multiply the number of pounds you weigh now by 15 calories. This number

represents the average number of calories used up in one day by a moderately active person of your weight. If you're sedentary, multiply your weight by 13.

To lose one pound, you need to burn 3500 calories more than you take in. In other words, you can reduce your caloric intake by 500 calories per day for seven days to lose one pound without endangering your health. Never cut back more than 500 calories per day.

Using the above example, a moderately active 150 pound person needs to consume about 2250 calories to maintain that weight. To lose one to two pounds a week without an increase in activity level, calorie intake should be cut back to about 1750 calories per day. Of course, this is just an estimate and will vary depending on each individual's metabolism.

The good news is that you can reduce the number of calories that need to be cut by increasing your activity level. If you burn an extra 250 calories a day, then you only need to reduce your caloric intake by 250 calories (250 less calories consumed plus 250 more calories burned equals a total daily reduction of 500 calories). Using a mix of exercise and caloric reduction is much less stressful to the body and therefor healthier than dieting alone. The addition of exercise also ensures that fat is being lost and not muscle tissue. In fact, not only will you lose fat through exercise, but you will build muscle and improve the health of your heart, a great additional reward for your hard work.

After 40 Fitness Tip

# of calories needed to
maintain your weight
=
your weight x 15

How to Lose Weight

The first step to losing weight is to monitor your eating habits. Keep a journal of what you eat, when, how much, where you eat it, what you are doing at the time and how you are feeling. This log can help you identify poor eating habits that stem not only from what you eat, but why you eat. Do you have a tendency to eat sugary foods when you are upset? Do you eat high fat foods when you are working late? To snack all day when you are home alone? By writing down your habits you can easily identify problem areas.

A few days of logging your eating habits should reveal where your problem areas lie. Are you eating a variety of foods from all of the food groups? Do you choose carbohydrates over fats when possible? Do you eat a light, nutritious breakfast? Do you eat a lot of fruits, vegetables and grains? Do you choose steamed or baked foods over fried or heavily sauced foods? Do you avoid high-fat foods? Foods to avoid include: hamburgers, steak, meat loaf, lunch meats, hot dogs, whole milk and cheese, cookies, cakes, donuts, fried foods, creams, gravies, chips, and ice cream. Occasionally indulging in fatty foods is fine, as long as they do not make up the bulk of your diet.

Of course, healthy eating habits should not equal starvation or deprivation of your favorite foods. The food guide pyramid recommends a daily diet of 6 to 11 servings of bread, cereal, rice or pasta; 2 to 4 servings of fruit; 3 to 5 servings of vegetables; and lesser servings of the other food groups with moderate intake of oils, fats and sweets. In fact, all three of the first food groups are good examples of foods that fill you up before they make you fat. Include plenty of fruits, vegetables and whole wheat foods in your diet to fill up and stay fit. You can get the protein you need from beans, grains and low fat dairy products instead of large portions of high-fat meat.

A simple rule of thumb to follow is to focus on the quality of food you eat first and the amount of food you eat second. Spread out your meals and always eat breakfast. A low fat breakfast jump-starts your metabolism and a series of 4 to 6 small meals during the day keeping it going in high gear. And remember to drink 6 to 8 glasses of water daily to stay properly hydrated for your martial arts training. When planning your diet, you may want to consult your doctor or a nutritionist to help you set realistic goals and understand what eating habits and nutritional supplements are right for you. These guidelines are offered as generally beneficial for healthy adults, but your needs may be different.

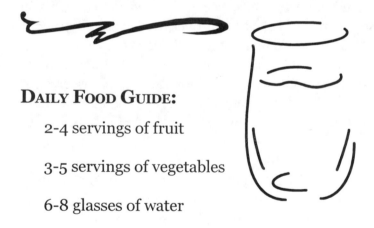

DAILY FOOD GUIDE:

2-4 servings of fruit

3-5 servings of vegetables

6-8 glasses of water

6-11 servings of bread, cereal, rice, pasta

lesser servings of meat and dairy products

small amounts of oils, fats and sweets

EXERCISE AS PART OF THE EQUATION

The type and duration of exercise you choose can have a big impact on the number of calories you burn. Choose activities, like martial arts for instance, that use the large muscles of the trunk, arms and legs. Movements like kicking and grappling that engage the whole body burn more calories than smaller range movements like practicing standing wrist locks.

The duration of exercise is also important. Somewhat contrary to common sense, exercising longer at a moderate pace is better than exercising briefly but very intensely. For example, running at a twelve minute mile pace would enable the average person to reasonably run three miles while running at a five minute mile pace would totally exhaust the average person at the one mile mark or less. Although both activities would probably leave you unable to continue exercising, you would have burned over 300 calories at the slow twelve minute pace and only a little over 100 calories at the five minute pace because the five minute pace forces you to quit exercising sooner. If your goal is burning the maximum amount of calories, choose longer duration moderate exercise whenever possible.

CHANGING YOUR EATING BEHAVIORS

There are two reasons we eat: we are hungry or we are subjected to an emotional or situational stimulus that triggers the desire to eat, often in the absence of hunger. If your analysis of your eating habits showed a pattern of frequently eating when you are not hungry, you may have to take steps to modify not only what you eat, but why you eat. Once you identify situations or emotions that trigger your desire to eat, devise replacement activities. For example, instead of going for the ice cream after an argument with a family member, go for a brisk walk or jog. Instead of munching on chips while watching TV, take up knitting, sewing, folding laundry or squeezing a squishy "stress buster" ball. Instead of snacking at 11:00 AM, run some errands that will keep you busy until lunch time. The main goal of this exercise is to create new, non-food related associations with the activities in your life that trigger the emotional desire to eat.

MAINTAINING YOUR TARGET WEIGHT

Once you have reached your target weight, continue to monitor your eating and exercise habits to stay at your goal weight. If you quickly reach your target weight, be careful to maintain a reduced caloric intake/increased caloric output for a while longer. Often, initial weight loss is due to water loss rather than fat loss and you may "rebound" if you return to your previous eating/exercise habits too soon after reaching your target weight. At least two months of maintaining your reduced weight is a good guideline to ensure that you have really lost fat.

To maintain your ideal weight, weigh yourself once a week at the same time of day and under the same conditions. For example, always get weighed on Saturday morning before breakfast wearing your pajamas. This will ensure that your reading is not affected by a meal or what you are wearing.

If you find that you are three to five pounds more than what you should be, start eating less or exercising more (or both) until your weight is back down to where you want it. If you lose too much weight, increase your caloric intake primarily by eating foods low in fat such as grains, vegetables, fruits and dairy products made with skim milk. Try to stay within five pounds of your goal weight.

Most importantly, be patient and keep your perspective. You are not going to do this for only one month. Remember that you are going to do this for the rest of your life.

The One Rule Diet

After 40 Fitness Tip

If you don't have the time or inclination to figure out how many calories you are eating or what balance of protein/fat/carbohydrates make up your diet then at least follow one simple rule: When you sit down to eat, think of your plate as a pie chart. Three quarters of your pie should consist of fruits, vegetables and grains. The rest should be rounded out with lean meat, fish and low fat dairy products. Following this rule and eating in moderation should keep you on the right track.

CALORIE INTAKE/OUTPUT BALANCE

No matter how you look at it, the calorie equation is deceptively simply. To illustrate the importance of balancing your daily calorie intake and output let's look at the effects of increasing one side of the equation. If, for example, you consume an additional 100 calories (one banana, say) per day and do not increase your daily energy expenditure, you will gain over 10 pounds in one year or over 50 pounds in five years! Why? Because 100 calories times 365 days equals 36,500 calories over the course of one year. If one pound of body fat contains 3,500 calories, 36,500 divided by 3,500 equals 10.4 pounds.

On the other hand if you consume 100 less calories per day and burn 100 more calories per day, by for example walking briskly for 30 minutes, you would reduce your body fat by 21 pounds in a year (assuming you have 21 pounds to lose). There are no magic tricks, special potions or miracle diets that can change this equation.

FUEL FOR ENDURANCE

If you are a recreational martial artist who goes to class a couple of times a week, your nutritional needs are pretty much the same as any other active, healthy adult. However, if you are training every day, training intensely for a few hours a day on successive days or training for competition, you may benefit from adjusting your diet to increase the amount of energy available to your muscles.

The nutrient that provides fuel to your muscles depends on the intensity and duration of exercise being done. During continuous, moderate exercise, the energy for muscular contraction is provided mainly by the body's fat and carbohydrate stores. If exercise continues to the point that glycogen stores in the muscles are greatly reduced, the supply of energy increasingly comes from the breakdown of stored fat. In this case, nutrients are dispersed through the blood stream to the working muscles to compensate for depleted glycogen supplies. During prolonged exercise, such as long distance running, the depletion of glycogen in the muscles can result in muscle fatigue, even though there is a large reserve of stored fat to be drawn upon. Once the muscles' fuel tank hits "empty" the potential for continued exercise is significantly inhibited.

A reduction in the glycogen levels in the muscles is often perceived by athletes as a feeling of being stale or having legs made of lead. This feeling usually occurs after a few consecutive days of hard training because muscle glycogen stores are not readily replenished to pre-exercise levels. In fact, it normally takes 48 hours to restore muscle glycogen levels in the muscles after prolonged, exhaustive exercise. To compensate for this effect, endurance athletes often practice carbohydrate loading, carefully moderating the level of exercise, carbohydrate intake and fat intake to deplete glycogen stores and then "pack" the muscles with glycogen prior to an event.

For martial artists, carbohydrate loading is of little benefit. Carbohydrate loading is more appropriate for marathon runners and triathletes who have to perform at maximum output for hours at a time. Martial artists, on the other hand, can benefit from consuming about 50 to 60% of the daily caloric intake in the form of carbohydrates. Fad diets that require low carbohydrate consumption combined with high protein or high fat consumption are not recommended for martial artists because low carbohydrate diets can lead to quick fatigue during exercise and an overall negative energy balance.

During a particularly intense period of training, such as prior to competition, carbohydrate intake may be increased to provide extra muscle glycogen. More important, though, is adequate rest so the body can replenish muscle glycogen stores between training sessions. Since muscle glycogen cannot be transferred between muscles and is only depleted when muscles are used, it is wise to alternate muscle groups during intense training, working the upper body one day and the lower body the next if you are intent on training every day.

PRECOMPETITION MEAL

Many martial artists compete in sparring, forms, breaking or weapons competition. A competition day may range from one form performance to several individual performances plus a number of sparring bouts. If you have a very intense day of competition planned, your pre-competition meal, normally breakfast, is a very important part of your day. The main purpose of the precompetition meal is to provide energy and optimal hydration. As a rule, foods high in fat should be avoided because fatty foods take longer to digest than foods with similar amounts of energy derived from carbohydrates.

The precompetition meal should be eaten at least three hours prior to the event to allow enough time for digestion and absorption. An appropriate precompetition meal is high in carbohydrates and low in fats and protein. Good choices breakfast include cereal, oatmeal, whole grain muffins or bagels, juice, skim milk, yogurt and/or fruit, all of which are easy on the stomach and provide much needed energy. Since martial arts competitions are often unpredictable in terms of scheduling, you should also plan to bring along healthy, easy to digest snacks like fruit, fruit juice, granola or protein bars and plenty of water to keep your energy levels up throughout the day. Never rely on buying snacks or even lunch at the tournament site because most tournaments sell high fat foods like hot dogs, pizza and French fries.

NEED TO BULK UP?

Although most adults over 40 are more interested in slimming down than in bulking up, you may find that you want to increase your muscle mass to benefit your martial arts training. If you are already in good shape, but find it difficult to increase your lean muscle mass, a few changes in your eating habits may show significant results. An increase in your protein intake, combined with a consistent strength training program can help build muscle mass. About 80 to 100 grams of protein per day are plenty for even a very active adult male. In general, you should avoid staying on a higher protein diet for extended periods because it is stressful on your kidneys.

Good sources of high quality protein include chicken breasts, tuna packed in water, tofu, white fish, yogurt, cottage cheese, beans, and skim milk. Although you can get added protein from supplement bars and drinks, they are an expensive methods of getting the same protein boost you can get from simply modifying your diet. In fact, you can make your own protein shake by combining 1.5 cups of skim milk, one banana and a half cup of fat free yogurt in the blender. Total protein: 16 grams of protein at only about one third the cost of commercial protein shakes.

Nutrition Tips

Eat only when you are hungry.

Eat the kinds of food you like.

Eat a variety of foods within each group.

Eat more complex-carbohydrates and fiber.

Eat more fish.

Eat vegetables and fruit.

Reduce fat (red meat, dairy products) consumption.

Avoid overusing salt, no more than 2,000 mg daily.

Avoid eating processed food.

Make good eating habits a part of your life.

WEIGHT CONTROL: THE BOTTOM LINE

Burn more calories than you consume.

You have three options:

Eat less.

Burn more.

Eat less and burn more.

THINKING POINTS

1. There are only two fundamental ways to lose weight burn more calories or eat less calories.

2. Dieting is a losing battle because it goes against the body's natural starvation defense system triggering weight gain as soon as the diet is stopped.

3. To maintain your present body weight, multiply your weight times 15. This is the number of calories you should eat daily.

4. Dieting alone can cause loss of muscle mass rather than fat.

5. A combination of increased exercise and decreased calorie consumption is the best way to control your weight.

6. Doing more exercise at a moderate pace is better for weight control than doing less exercise at a strenuous pace.

7. Carbohydrate loading and high protein diets are not beneficial for recreational martial artists.

8. Before competition, eat a meal high in carbohydrates and low in fat and protein at least three hours before your first event.

chapter 4

Choosing Fitness

Often, after you hit 40, your body begins to send messages—
stiffening muscles and creaking joints. Much of the decline
of physical ability and health associated with aging is, in fact,
accelerated by inactivity. One of the characteristics of aging
is a loss of muscle mass and strength. The other aspect of
aging is that the cells in your body become inefficient in
utilizing oxygen. When these things are happening to you,
your body is telling you something important.

Heart-related disease and cancer account for nearly seventy
percent of all deaths in America. Obesity and heredity are the
primary factors for these fatalities. The good news is that the
former can be reduced. It is a matter of certain choices that
you make in your life. Do you smoke? Would you like to be
overweight? Do you want to be stressed out? The bottom line
is that you have options. Whether you have been brought up
in a family eating fatty foods everyday for 40 years, or you
like to eat junk and to smoke, it is your free choice. Either

you break the habits deeply rooted in your daily life or you live the rest of your life avoiding painful realities. It's entirely in your hands.

For any pain, there are many drugs out there that can easily mask the causes of your problems. There is a variety of drugs for backaches, ulcers, weight control, and high blood pressure. But eventually you will hit the reality that none of the drugs can do much. The best solution for your health is exercise.

Your choice changes your outlook. A different outlook brings a different life-style. The moment you sense the problem, you can choose which way to go. Imagine what kind of life you want to have next year. What will you be look like? How will you feel about yourself in 5 years? Will you like the way you are now or do you think you need some changes in your current life-style?

The choice is yours. Enjoy being fit!

SUCCESS TIPS FOR ULTIMATE FITNESS AFTER 40

Before you Begin a Fitness Program

· Check with your doctor for a risk-factor analysis before
  you begin any new physical activities including martial
  arts.

· Familiarize yourself with the fundamentals of exercise.
  Know which exercises may be harmful, especially if you
  have a prior injury or pre-existing condition.

· Choose activities that are fun, not exhausting. Enjoy your
  training.

· Add variety. Try not to rely too much on one activity,
  but develop a repertoire of several that you can enjoy.
  That way, training will never seem boring or routine.
  You can work within your martial art, practicing forms,
  sparring, weapons, etc. for variety or try cross training in
  other activities like jogging, swimming or cycling.

· Wear comfortable, properly fitted footwear and comfortable, loose-fitting clothing that is appropriate for the
  weather and the activity.

· Find a convenient time and place to workout. Try to
  make it a habit, but be flexible. If you miss a workout,
  squeeze some activity into your day another way.

· Surround yourself with supportive people. Decide what kind of support you need. Do you want them to remind you to go to class? Ask about your progress? Participate with you regularly or occasionally? Allow you time to exercise by yourself? Go with you to a special event, such as a tournament or demonstration? Be understanding when you get up early to go to class? Spend time with the children while you are at class?

· Learn and practice efficient problem-solving techniques, so that you can get over obstacles and compromise tough situations.

· Determine who is in control of your daily life. Make sure bad habits don't take over your life.

· Practice sensible eating habits.

During your Workout

· Warm up and cool down at every workout.

· Know your target heart rate and do not go over it. (Subtract 17 beats from you target heart rate when exercising in the water.)

· Stop when you feel fatigued. Adjust your expectations if necessary.

· Adjust the intensity of your training according to your current condition. When you are having a bad day, go back to basics and take it easy.

· Surround yourself with highly motivated people.

· Share your activity with others. Attending group martial arts classes is a great motivator to stay on a regular schedule.

· Use music to keep yourself entertained when you work-out alone.

· Don't overdo it. You can slowly increase the duration and intensity of your activities as you become more fit. Over time, work up to exercising three or four times per week for 30-60 minutes.

· Focus on one or two areas of training that you can be good at and work on them.

· Take progressive steps to improving yourself.

· Be sensible and patient in your training.

After Every Workout

· Have a sufficient recovery period after exercise. Train every other day or alternate intense and light workouts.

· Keep a record of your activities. Reward yourself at special milestones. Nothing motivates like success!

· Don't compare yourself to others—especially the teenagers in class. Check your own progress.

- Give credit yourself credit for effort. Don't be too hard on yourself.

- Learn to anticipate, avoid and cope with stressful situations.

- Practice deep breathing exercises regularly.

- Be positive no matter what.

- Live your life to the fullest.

SIX STEPS TO A HEALTHIER MIND

1. Recognize your potential.

2. Identify your strengths and weaknesses.

3. Accept your weaknesses, and develop your strengths.

4. Adjust your expectations.

5. Be realistic about what you can do.

6. Check your progress and reward yourself.

101 THINGS THAT YOU CAN DO

EVERY DAY TO IMPROVE YOUR FITNESS!

Fitness at your Desk

Stretch your legs all the way forward and contract your leg muscles five times.

Stretch your arms up and hold your hands together, hold 15 seconds three times.

Cross your fingers and stretch them out palm facing forward, raise them, and put them behind your head, and stretch your back.

Put both palms together in front of you, and push hard ten times.

Put your hands on your waist, squeeze your body five times.

Bring your left arm in front of your neck with your elbow bent and your left hand resting on your right shoulder, gently push the elbow with your right hand.

Turn your head to the left and right ten times.

Circulate your shoulders forward and backward ten times each, with arms resting at your sides.

Push your chair back and touch your feet with your hands.

Bring your left knee up straight and pull it tight toward the chest and repeat with the other leg.

Bring your ankle on the knee of the other leg horizontally and pull it. Alternate legs five times.

Rotate your ankle left and right for 15 seconds.

Sit straight and breath deeply for one minute.

Sit straight and look back slowly to the left and right. Repeat ten times.

Sit straight and bend your torso slowly to the left and right five times each.

Stretch both arms sideways, grasp the sides of your desk and squeeze inward.

Put both hands under your desk and push it up as you try to lift it.

Push your desk away from you with fingers.

Fitness on the Go

Brainstorm project ideas with a co-worker while taking a walk instead of sitting at your desk.

Stand while talking on the telephone.

Walk down the hall to speak with someone rather than using the telephone.

Take the stairs instead of the elevator.

Get off the elevator a few floors early and take the stairs the remainder of the way.

Walk around while waiting for a plane at the airport.

Stay at hotels with fitness centers or swimming pools while on business trips.

Take along a jump rope in your suitcase when you travel. Jump rope and do calisthenics in your hotel room.

Participate in or start a recreation league at your company.

Form a sports team to raise money for charity events.

Join a fitness center at or near your work place, and work out before or after work to avoid rush hour traffic.

Drop by the gym for a noon workout.

Schedule your exercise time on your business calendar and treat it as any other important appointment.

Get off the bus a few blocks early and walk the rest of the way to work or home.

Walk around your building for a break during the work day or during lunch.

Home Fitness

Watch TV while holding one leg one foot above from the floor for 30 seconds. Alternate legs.

Watch TV while raising and lowering a five pound weight in one hand. Alternate hands.

Watch TV on the floor in mid-sit-up position for one minute (No need to do sit-ups).

Watch TV in Sumo squat position for 30 seconds x three sets.

Watch TV in push-up position for one minute (No need to do push-ups).

Ride a stationary bike while watching TV.

Do calisthenics during commercial breaks..

Do shadow boxing for one minute x three rounds between TV shows.

Walk or jog in place during commercials.

Do housework.

Mow the grass.

Rearrange a flower bed.

Rake leaves.

Prune trees.

Dig.

Pick up trash.

Go out for a short walk before breakfast and after dinner.

Walk or bike to the corner store instead of driving.

When walking, pick up the pace from leisurely to brisk. Choose a hilly route.

Instead of asking someone to bring you a drink, get up off the couch and get it yourself.

Pace around the room while talking on the telephone.

Walk the dog.

Park farther away at the shopping mall and walk the extra distance.

Walk an extra lap or two around the mall.

Stretch to reach items in high places.

Squat to look at items at floor level.

Bend to pick up dirt on the rug.

Clean your windows inside and out.

Outdoor Fitness

Hike.

Swim.

Dance.

Dance faster.

Kick to music.

Practice forms in your back yard or the park.

Stretch.

Practice stick combat with the trees in the woods.

Backpack.

Walk a scenic trail.

Jog through the woods.

Bike a challenging route.

Make a friend who enjoys your favorite physical activities. Do them regularly together.

Play motivating music while exercising.

Join a recreational club.

At the beach, sit and watch the waves.

Get up and walk in the shallow water.

Run along the beach.

Play in the surf.

Play beach ball.

Play badminton.

Kick or punch under water.

When golfing, walk instead of using a cart.

Play singles racquetball.

Play singles tennis instead of doubles.

Canoe.

Row a boat.

Play a little every day.

Book II

GET FIGHTING FIT
AND STAY THAT WAY

chapter 5

Fitness Attributes
After 40

For the average person, the performance capacity of the human body improves rapidly from early childhood and peaks between the ages of twenty and thirty. Thereafter, attributes like strength, flexibility and reflexes begin a steady decline. Although this trend holds true for both active and sedentary people, an active person may peak at a much higher functional capacity and while he might decline at the same rate, his functional capacity at fifty might be same as a sedentary person's capacity at twenty-five.

To illustrate this point, imagine that an active martial artists peaks in his late twenties at a physiologic functional capacity of 120% and a sedentary adult peaks in his twenties at a functional capacity of 95%. Although both experience a similar rate of decline as they age, the active martial artist will be going strong at about 100% functional capacity at age 50 while the sedentary man will have dropped to 75% at the same age. In other words, the active martial artist will be in better shape at age 50 than a sedentary person of half his age.

Before we look at how to improve your physical attributes for martial arts training, let's take a look at how aging affects the functional capacity of the body over time.

STRENGTH

Maximum adult strength is generally achieved between the ages of 20 and 30 years old. Muscular strength naturally declines thereafter at a rate of about three to five percent per decade, leading to as much as thirty percent loss of muscular strength by age seventy. The good news: this loss of muscular strength is almost entirely due to a loss of muscle protein brought on by inactivity or aging. Studies have shown that regular physical training facilitates protein retention and strength maintenance. In fact, adults over the age of thirty can not only stop the decline, but they can make great gains in muscular strength and endurance through regular strength training.

FLEXIBILITY

As the body ages, connective tissue (ligaments, cartilage and tendons) becomes more rigid and reduces joint flexibility. Much of this decline may be due to inactivity rather than aging. A regular program of stretching can lead to increased flexibility and range of motion at any age.

REFLEXES

The aging process takes a harsh toll on the central nervous system and decreases reaction time as the years go by. While you cannot physically stretch or strengthen the connection between your brain and body, you can slow the loss of quick reflexes through regular exercise and participation in activities that require communication between your brain and muscles.

Martial arts, in all forms, is an excellent neuro-muscular workout.

ENDURANCE

Maximal oxygen consumption and endurance performance decline steadily between the ages of 20 and 65, resulting in an overall loss of about 35% of aerobic endurance capacity by age 65. The heart's ability to pump blood decreases about eight percent per decade and the maximal heart rate progressively declines as we age. Again, the good news is that it is uncertain whether aging is to blame or these changes are attributable to a sedentary life style. Studies have shown that sedentary adults can suffer losses in functional capacity that far exceed the effects of aging itself. On the other hand, studies have also shown that there is virtually no loss in aerobic capacity for middle age adults who follow a regular cardiovascular conditioning program. Some adults in these studies were able to maintain the same aerobic capacity and blood pressure for over ten years.

ATTRIBUTES VS. SKILLS

There are two components to martial arts training: the development of attributes and the development of skills. Attributes include physical qualities such as flexibility, strength and endurance. Skills include learned motor movements like kicking and punching. The development of skills will be severely limited if the development of attributes is neglected. However, attributes can easily be developed exclusive of skills. Of course developing attributes without skills falls into the realm of calisthenics, not martial arts.

In the early stages of learning a martial art, the very practice of skills may serve to develop a wide range of attributes including flexibility, strength, coordination, reflexes and endurance. As you become more adept and your physical condition improves, you may have to develop certain attributes independent of skill practice by devoting time each training period specifically to conditioning exercises.

For example, when you first learn a front kick you may progress rapidly in the technical development and performance of the kick up to chest height. At some point, you will want to kick harder, higher or faster but cannot seem to make any further gains through practice of the kick alone. At this juncture, the addition of flexibility or strengthening exercises for your legs will directly contribute to the further development of your kicking skills. Similarly, when you first begin taking lessons, the strenuousness of class itself may be enough to give you a good cardio workout. As your cardiovascular capacity improves, class will begin to seem easy and you may find the need to supplement your class time with additional cardio workouts such as jogging or cycling.

Conversely, you may find that your attribute development is hindering your skill development if your conditioning plan is not specifically designed for martial arts. If you are running nearly fifty miles a week for cardiovascular conditioning, you may find that the speed of your kicks suffers because you are developing endurance related slow twitch muscle fibers in your legs rather than the more explosive fast twitch muscle fibers.

Thinking Points

1. It is possible for a 50 year old to be as fit as a 25 year old, in spite of the natural decline in physiologic functional capacity.

2. Although muscular strength can decline as much as three to five percent per decade, most of this decline can be offset through regular strength training.

3. A regular program of stretching can lead to increased flexibility at any age.

4. Martial arts training requires the development of both attributes and skills. Skills can be developed independently of attributes, but this may limit progress.

5. Attribute training should be structured with the end result in mind. Attribute training that most closely resembles the martial arts skills to be practiced is more beneficial than general attribute training.

chapter 6

Agility after 40

Agility is the ability to physically adapt to changing conditions. It is most associated with young football players and gymnasts, but can be developed well into middle age with practice. Agility is often confused with coordination, yet it is more than coordination. Agility is a kind of physical intelligence that blends coordination, perception, speed, strength and balance.

The very act of learning new martial arts skills on a regular basis will improve your agility and it's cousin, your coordination. Agility can also be increased through playing martial arts games or through sparring. Any activity that requires you to smoothly string together groups of movements or skills develops agility. As you age, flexibility and strength play increasingly important roles in maintaining your agility. The following exercises can be integrated into your martial arts training to improve or maintain your agility.

Agility Exercises

*You may vary the height, intensity and frequency of the following exercises according to your current fitness level.

A-1 JUMPING DRILLS

Execution: Jump up and touch your knees to your chest or jump up and touch your feet to your buttocks.

Fitness benefits: Improves upper-lower body coordination, flexibility and leg strength.

Martial arts benefits: Improves jumping kicks and leg strength for grappling.

A-2   ZIG-ZAG RUN

Execution: Run 50 to 100 yards in a zig-zag pattern.

Fitness benefits: Total body agility, coordination, speed

Martial arts benefits: Improves footwork and body shifting.

A-3   SHUTTLE RUN

Execution: Mark off two lines on the ground, ten to twenty yards apart. Start at one line and sprint to the other, bend to touch it and sprint back to the first line.

Fitness benefits: Total body agility, endurance and speed

Martial arts benefits: Improves footwork and changing heights (for grappling).

Cautions: Do not do this exercise if you have a pre-existing ankle or knee injury. The touch down and turn phase of this exercise places a great deal of stress on the lead leg, ankle, and knee.

A-4 FOOTWORK DRILLS

Execution: For one minute, bounce on both feet alternating moving forward-backward and side to side. Rest thirty seconds, then for one minute slide right to left and forward-backward alternately.

Fitness benefits: Total body agility, coordination, mobility, leg strength and balance

Martial arts benefits: Improves body shifting and footwork.

A-5 SHADOW SPARRING

Execution: Spar with an imaginary opponent for a one to three minute round. Rest thirty to sixty seconds. Repeat three times.

Fitness benefits: Improves total body agility, coordination, timing and balance.

Martial arts benefits: Improves sparring skills, combinations and flow of techniques.

A-6 SHOULDER STANDING

Execution: Lie on your back. Raise your legs toward the ceiling, transferring your weight onto your upper back and shoulders. Place your hands on your hips for supper.

Fitness benefits: Improves total body agility, flexibility and balance.

Martial arts benefits: Strength and flexibility for falling and grappling skills

Cautions: Do not do this exercise if you have a pre-existing neck or back injury. Stop if you experience neck or back pain.

A-7 SPINAL ROLL

Execution: Sit with your knees drawn up to your chest and your hands around clasped around your thighs. Roll backward and extend your legs straight over your head so your feet touch the ground above your head.

Fitness benefits: Total body agility and flexibility

Martial arts benefits: Improves strength and flexibility for falling and grappling.

Cautions: Do not do this exercise if you have a pre-existing neck or back injury. Stop if you experience neck or back pain.

A-8 LEG RAISES

Execution: Standing on one leg, lift the other leg slowly up to the front. Lower it and without pausing, raise it slowly up to the rear. Lower it and without pausing raise it slowly out to the side.

Fitness benefits: Lower body agility, flexibility and balance

Martial arts benefits: Balance for kicking and throwing

A-9 ROPE LADDER DRILLS

Execution: This drill can be done using a rope ladder laid on the floor or tape marking off twelve inch segments for a ten to twenty foot length. Run briskly down the length of the ladder, taking one step only in each segment. Move as quickly as you can without touching the ladder rungs or tape.

You can also run sideways, hop sideways or hop forward. A very advanced variation is to stand next to the ladder. Step into one segment with one foot then the other. Quickly step out of that segment with one foot then the other. Repeat with each segment, moving quickly into and out of the ladder as you work your way down it. This variation can be done facing the ladder or parallel to it.

Fitness benefits: Total body agility, speed and coordination

Martial arts benefits: Quick change of direction, foot speed, and lower body coordination for sparring

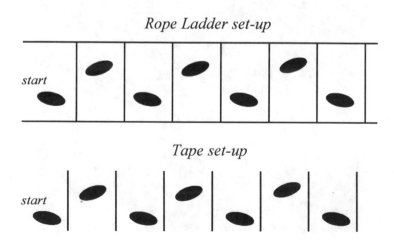

Rope Ladder set-up

Tape set-up

THINKING POINTS

1. Agility is the ability to physically adapt to changing conditions.

2. Agility blends coordination, perception, speed, strength and balance.

3. Martial arts practice can significantly improve agility.

4. Additional agility improvements can be made through playing martial arts games, sparring or combination practice.

5. Flexibility plays an important role in agility and should be developed concurrently.

chapter 7

Flexibility after 40

While the average forty year old thinks stretching is the
equivalent of being drawn and quartered, martial artists know
better. In fact, if you've been practicing the martial arts for a
few years or more, you are probably quite flexible, much more
flexible than others your age. But you may also be feeling the
effects of time, meaning you are not as flexible as you were
five years ago. As part of the natural aging process, the joints
tighten and the muscles shorten. But the good news is that
much of this process is the result of life-style rather than age.
In other words, you can delay or even prevent tightness with
a regular program of stretching and strengthening. You may
even be able to achieve greater flexibility than before you
started martial arts.

CONVENTIONAL STRETCHING METHODS

Stretching is actually counterintuitive to your body. When you stretch a muscle, the body's natural reaction is to tighten and try to shorten the muscle. Fortunately, there is structure located at the junction of the tendons and muscles, called the golgi tendon organ, which sends a message to the muscle to relax and lengthen further if the stretch is held long enough. Stretching and holding a stretch for 20 to 30 seconds is called static stretching, which is the safest, most often recommended method of stretching. In fact, studies have shown that the majority of muscle relaxation occurs within 20 seconds of stretching. By stretching, holding for 20 seconds, relaxing and then beginning again, you will see steady gains with a very low risk of injury.

ADVANCED STRETCHING METHODS

If you are very flexible and in good shape, you may wish to investigate other, more advanced methods of stretching like PNF (proprioceptive neuromuscular facilitation) and AI (active isolated) stretching. PNF stretching involves exerting downward pressure on the muscle you're stretching while a partner holds the limb being stretched to provide resistance. For example, from a standing position, you partner raises your leg in an extended side kick, supporting your ankle or calf. Once you reach a comfortable stretch, you exert downward pressure against your partner's hand for a few seconds while he holds your leg steady. Release and repeat this contraction a few times, increasing the height of the stretch if you can, before moving on to another position.

AI stretching involves contracting the antagonist (opposing, for example, hamstring and quadriceps muscles) muscle just prior to stretching. Because AI and PNF stretching should be undertaken under the supervision of a qualified trainer and have a higher risk of injury than static stretching if done wrong, they are not discussed in detail this section. If you want to pursue advanced methods of flexibility training, consult a personal trainer or sports specialist for instruction before you begin.

MAXIMIZING YOUR STRETCHING GAINS

When stretching to increase your flexibility, always warm-up first by doing some basic aerobic exercise for five to ten minutes or until you break a light sweat. In fact, many martial artists realize the best gains by doing deep stretching near the end of class. Keep in mind that the stretching done to increase flexibility is different from the stretching done to prepare your body for activity at the start of class. Once you have thoroughly warmed up, you can push your body harder and stretch more deeply than at the beginning of a workout when you are just working toward an overall loosening of the major muscle groups.

Whenever you stretch, be sure to breathe deeply with each movement. Breathe in deeply and exhale as you lower your body into a stretch. As you hold your stretch, breathe lightly and naturally. Never hold your breath while stretching. If you cannot breathe naturally, you are stretching too hard. Avoid pushing yourself too hard or competing with other students to see who is more flexible. Some people are naturally more flexible overall or in certain body parts. In fact, women, in general, are more flexible than men, especially in the hips and legs. Always compare yourself only to yourself. As long as you are seeing steady improvements each week, you are on the right track.

Try to stretch in a warm environment. If you are cold, you will find stretching more difficult. If the class room is cool, do some extra aerobic activity to raise your body temperature.

FUNCTIONAL FLEXIBILITY

A final important note with regard to stretching is that you should differentiate between functional flexibility and flexibility for its own sake. Many martial artists fall into the trap of stretching for the sake of stretching, trying to do full splits or touch their head to their knees. While this is a measurable form of flexibility, it is not necessarily useful in your day to day martial arts training. If you can do a full split by using tricks like rolling your hips, but you cannot kick more than chest high, your stretching efforts are not productive. Functional flexibility means stretching to improve the height or range of motion in your techniques, not to perform static tests of flexibility like splits.

Functional flexibility entails stretching in ways that directly contribute to your martial arts training, for example stretching at the bar in side kick position. This type of stretching directly involves the muscles you use for kicking in the same position that you use them. You can also improve your functional flexibility by doing gentle low power techniques, such as kicking, striking or throwing while concentrating solely on lengthening your range of motion throughout the performance of the technique. Always practice this type of dynamic stretching after you have fully warmed up and work at half power or less.

. . . .

STRETCHING PRECAUTIONS:

Of all the types of attribute training, flexibility is the one most commonly done incorrectly, resulting in nagging injuries and reduced flexibility. The following are some precautions to keep in mind when stretching:

1. Never bounce during a stretch.
Move slowly into each stretch, hold for ten to twenty seconds and return to a relaxed position.

2. Keep your back straight.
Always keep your spine straight and bend from your hips during stretches.

3. Never bend your knees more than ninety degrees during squats.
If you have had previous knee problems, do not bend your knees more than ninety degrees during any standing flexibility exercise. Do bent knee stretches while seated, and then only to the degree that you do not have knee pain.

4. Be patient.
You cannot force flexibility. It comes over time with gradual consistent progress. Avoid comparing yourself to others in class, even if they are your age or older. Everyone's body is different, especially when it comes to flexibility. Pushing yourself too hard may result in more pain than gain.

5. Feel the burn.

Effective stretches should cause a slight, but not intolerable, burn in your muscles. As long as you are feeling tension during the maximum point of the stretch, you are improving your flexibility. If you find the stretch is causing intolerable pain in your muscles or joints, you are pushing too hard. Ease up a bit on the tension to make it bearable.

6. Don't cheat.

Focus on maintaining correct posture during a stretch so you gain it's full benefit. Bending your knees so you can touch the ground during a toe touch doesn't improve your flexibility, even if it does inflate your ego.

7. Work within your genetic limitations.

Not everyone is genetically predisposed to doing a full split, kicking over the head or touching their toes. You may find that no matter how hard you try, you just cannot kick above chest height. Perhaps you are quite flexible in your legs, but your hip structure is not conducive to high kicks. Don't let yourself get fixated on any one aspect of stretching or compare yourself to others. Look for overall gains in flexibility rather than forcing yourself to meet one hundred percent of your goals.

8. Stretch all major muscle groups at each workout.

Just because your shoulders don't feel as tight as your legs, you should not skip stretching your shoulder muscles. In addition to improving your flexibility, stretching at the start of a workout prepares your body for activity and can prevent muscle, joint, ligament and tendon injuries.

9. Differentiate between stretching for flexibility and stretching to warm-up.
You should lightly stretch before every workout to warm-up and prepare your muscles for activity. Hard stretching, to gain flexibility, should be done no more than three times a week on alternating days. Hard stretching is the stretching you do during or at the end of your workout after your muscles are warm and pliable. Recovering from hard stretching can take 24 to 72 hours, with your recovery time lengthening as you age.

10. Avoid exercises that cause joint pain or feel uncomfortable.
You don't need to do dozens of stretches, just pick one for each area of your body and do it consistently. The exercises pictured in this chapter cover the major muscles groups and are relatively low risk. Start here and add other exercises that you like to create a daily stretching routine you are comfortable with.

Flexibility Exercises

*You may vary the height, intensity and frequency of the following exercises according to your current fitness level.

F-1 NECK STRETCH

Execution: Beginning at the right shoulder, slowly rotate the head across the chest and to the left shoulder. Look up and then down.

Fitness benefits: Prepares the neck for exercise.

Martial arts benefits: Increases flexibility in turning movements and during falls or rolls.

F-2 ARM CIRCLES

Execution: Extend the arms straight out to the sides. Rotate slowly in large circles to the front and then to the back. Next rotate in small circles to the front and then to the back.

Fitness benefits: Prepares the shoulders for exercise.

Martial arts benefits: Increases range of motion for circular striking and throwing movements.

F-3 ARM RAISES

Execution: Stand with your feet a bit more than shoulder width apart and your fists on the ground. Keep your back straight and bend from the waist. Extend your right arm up above your back while keeping your left fist on the ground. Alternate sides.

Fitness benefits: Prepares the shoulders, chest and torso for exercise.

Martial arts benefits: Improves flexibility for twisting, throwing and striking movements.

F-4 FOREARM STRETCHES

Execution: Grasp the fingers of your right hand with your left hand and pull towards you. Push on the back of your hand, pressing towards your elbow.

Fitness benefits: Prepares the wrist and forearm for exercise.

Martial arts benefits: Increases range of motion for grappling, joint locking and weapons skills.

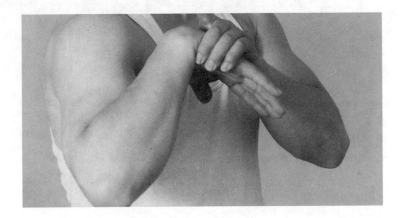

F-5 FINGER PRESS

Execution: Stretch your arms in front of you and interlock your fingers with your thumbs facing downwards. Stretch and flex your elbows.

Fitness benefits: Stretches the fingers and wrist.

Martial arts benefits: Improves strength and flexibility for grappling, grabbing and gripping a weapon

F-6 SEATED TRUNK TWIST

Execution: Sit with your left leg crossed over your right leg and your right arm on your left leg. Twist your upper body to the right. Alternate sides.

Fitness benefits: Improves trunk flexibility.

Martial arts benefits: Improves range of motion for striking, throwing and spinning skills.

F-7 SIDE BENDS

Execution: Standing, raise one arm and stretch it over your head while you bend to the side.

Fitness benefits: Stretches the side (oblique) muscles.

Martial arts benefits: Improves range of motion for striking and throwing techniques.

F-8 BACK STRETCH

Execution: Kneel and lean forward, stretching your arms above your head.

Fitness benefits: Prepares the back for exercise.

Martial arts benefits: Improves range of motion for kicking, striking and grappling skills.

F-9 BACK ROLL

Execution: Sit with your knees bent and your hands clasped around your thighs. Gently roll back until your shoulder blades touch the floor and then roll up to the starting position.

Fitness benefits: Prepares the back for exercise.

Martial arts benefits: Stretches and strengthens the spinal column area for falling and throwing.

F-10 KNEE ROTATION

Execution: Stand with both knees together. Place your hands on your knees and rotate clockwise and then counterclockwise.

Fitness benefits: Prepares the knees for exercise.

Martial arts benefits: Good warm-up for kicking and footwork.

F-11 TOE TOUCH

Execution: Stand with the feet together and knees straight. Bend at the waist and touch your hands to your toes or to the floor.

Fitness benefits: Improves back, buttock and hamstring flexibility

Martial arts benefits: Improves kicking height and stance depth.

F-12 GROIN STRETCH

Execution: Stand with your feet about twice your shoulder's width apart. Squat to the side with one leg bent and the other extended to the side. Stand up slowly and alternate sides.

Fitness benefits: Stretches the groin and thigh muscles

Martial arts benefits: Improves kicking height and range.

Cautions: Do not do this exercise if you have a pre-existing knee injury.

F-13 KNEE RAISES

Execution: Stand with your feet shoulder width apart. Raise your knee up as high as you can. Alternate sides. For an added benefit, twist to touch your knee to the opposite elbow.

Fitness benefits: Stretches hips, back, and hamstrings

Martial arts benefits: Improves kicking height, strength and range as well as leg and abdomen strength.

F-14 LEG EXTENSIONS

Execution: Lying on your back, grasp the arch of your right foot with your right hand. Extend your right leg and pull toward your head.

Fitness benefits: Stretches the hamstrings and buttocks.

Martial arts benefits: Improves kicking height and range of motion.

F-15 ANKLE ROTATION

Execution: Sit with your right leg extended and your left leg resting on it. Grasp your left foot and gently rotate your ankle clockwise and counterclockwise.

Fitness benefits: Prepares the ankle for exercise.

Martial arts benefits: Good warm-up for footwork and jumping.

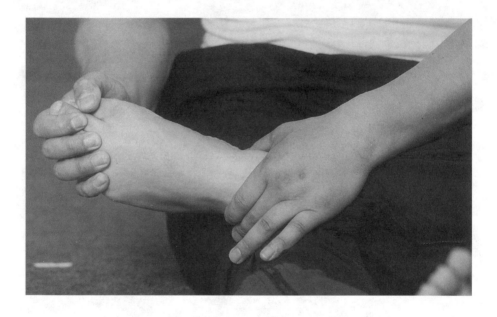

THINKING POINTS

1. Stretching has two functions in martial arts training: to prepare the muscles for exercise and to increase flexibility.

2. Stretches are most beneficial when held for twenty to thirty seconds.

3. Advanced stretching methods may be used by those in good physical condition under the instruction of a trainer to produce further gains in flexibility once the benefits of static stretching have been realized.

4. Stretching for flexibility gains is most beneficial after a period of aerobic exercise warms the muscles. Many martial artists prefer to stretch for flexibility at the end of a workout or class.

5. Never hold your breath during stretches. Always breathe in deeply before a stretch and exhale as you lower into the stretch.

6. Emphasize functional flexibility and be happy with reaching a majority of your goals. Do not force yourself to meet goals that are not right for your body shape or composition.

7. Never bounce during a stretch. Stretch slowly, until you feel a pulling or burning sensation and hold for at least twenty seconds.

8. Stretch all of the major muscle groups at every work out.

9. Avoid stretches that cause joint pain.

Power after 40

There are two primary types of strengthening exercises: Isometric (static) and Isotonic (dynamic).

Isometric exercise is defined as a muscular contraction with no noticeable shortening of the muscle (without movement) such as pushing against an immovable wall. Isometric exercise does not require any equipment, just an immovable surface, such as a wall, couch, heavy table or a friend to provide resistance. Some martial artists using isometric exercise to increase the strength of their strikes or kicks by applying force against a wall with the kick or strike fully extended and holding for 5 to 10 seconds. Isometric contractions are most effective when done five to seven times because after the third repetition, the muscles begin to fatigue and the benefits of the exercise decrease.

However, you shouldn't expect huge muscle gains from isometric exercise because it strengthens muscles in one position only - the position of contraction. This is a very inefficient method of strength training when other means, such as isotonic strength training are available. However, isometric exercise can be a valuable part of a rehabilitation program for joint injuries because it works your muscles without stressing your joints.

Isotonic exercise is defined as muscular contraction resulting in the lengthening or shortening of the muscles (movement), such as rip cord training or weight lifting. While weight lifting is a good supplement to martial arts training, many martial artists are increasingly learning the benefits of rip-cord or thera-band training. This is a form of isotonic exercise in which you attach one end of a piece of resistive elastic tubing (either by holding it in your hand or by Velcro strapping it to your ankle) to your body and attach the other end to a fixed object like a pole or wall. If you have a willing training partner, you can take turns holding one end to provide variable resistance.

With the resistive tubing firmly in place, you can execute punches, strikes, throws, and kicks while the elastic provides resistance for your muscles. The advantage over weight training is that you are directly working the muscles you use in your martial arts training, thereby guaranteeing targeted results. The drawbacks are that it may be difficult to find the right strength tubing, that it may be difficult to improve progressively, and that many kicks/strikes are not suited to this type of training because of the risk of injury.

In addition to resistance training, there are many strength building exercises than can be done with little or no equipment for martial artists who do not have access to weights or weight training equipment. A selection of strengthening exercises with excellent martial arts benefits is included at the end of this chapter.

WEIGHT TRAINING

Training for sheer muscular strength is done with high resistance (hundreds of pounds of weight) and low repetitions (three to five) in two to three sets. Muscular endurance training is done with lower resistance (half of your maximum) and high repetitions (25 to thirty reps per set) done as quickly as possible. For martial arts training, a middle ground is most beneficial.

If you plan to supplement your martial arts training with weight training, choose a weight which allows you to do about eight to twelve repetitions, with the last repetition being very hard to complete. If you cannot do at least eight repetitions, the weight you chose is too heavy. Begin with one set and gradually work up to three sets in a workout. Once you reach three sets, cut back your sets and increase your weight. Like all types of conditioning exercises, weight training requires one day of rest between sessions to allow your muscles to recover and rebuild. To prevent your muscles from becoming tight, stretch all of the muscles worked before and after every weight training session. For specific weight training exercises and instructions, consult a weight training guide like *Weight Training for Martial Artists* from Turtle Press.

SPECIFICITY IN STRENGTH TRAINING

Strength training for a specific activity, such as martial arts, requires more than just identifying and overloading the muscles involved through weight training. It requires that training be specific to the movements you use in the activity. If you are doing strength training for overall fitness, you can choose whatever strength training exercises you like most. However, if you are training for a specific outcome, such as stronger punches, you have to choose exercises that can produce the desired outcome.

The best method of strength training for martial arts is to train the muscles with movements as similar as possible to those in the actual skill. Good examples of this rule are light punching while holding hand weights, kicking using a rip cord or throwing using a bike inner tube for resistance. An important caution when using strength training equipment during martial arts movements is to avoid over-stressing the joints. Wearing ankle weights while doing full power kicks is a sure way to seriously injure your knees. Instead, try very slow, controlled kicks (with one hand against a wall for support if needed) while wearing ankle weights.

PLANNING YOUR STRENGTH TRAINING

There are five steps to creating a strength training plan:

1. *Establish your objectives:*

What is your goal? How will you measure results? By asking these two questions, you can narrow down the scope of your training plan. As a martial artist, you are probably interested in increasing your power and speed while maintaining or improving your flexibility. This is a very different strength training goal than a college football player who wants to bulk up or an Olympic power lifter.

Once you have a specific goal in mind, you should create a training program that promotes total body strength with an emphasis on your goals. Avoid training only one area of your body such as your chest or legs. The martial arts are a total body activity. Stronger punches are created through stronger arm, chest, shoulder, back and leg muscles. Stronger kicks are created through stronger leg, back and abdomen muscles. Keep your training plan focused but balanced.

2. *Schedule your workouts:*

A basic set of strengthening exercises can be completed in as little as 15 minutes. If your strength training is a supplement of your martial arts classes, you can probably do two sessions a week and still see positive gains. If you have trouble finding time for strength training, try to fit it in right after your martial arts class. This helps create a routine and saves time by eliminating the need for a warm-up.

3. *Gather your equipment:*

You may have access to strength training equipment at your martial art school. If you do, take full advantage of this convenient, low cost option. If not, you can develop a complete strength training program with a low cost set of barbells or other common household objects. If funds are tight, use your imagination. Jugs of water, bricks, telephone books, or old socks filled with sand can double for dumbbells. A broom handle with pails of sand attached to the ends can fill in for a barbell. And there are plenty of strength training exercises, like push-ups, sit-ups and leg lifts that require no equipment at all.

4. *Choose your exercises:*

Based on your goals, the amount of time you have and the equipment available, choose the exercises you will use. Remember, it is best to choose exercises that most closely relate to your martial arts training first. Once you have chosen a set of exercises, you should be certain you are doing them correctly. Proper form can significantly affect your strength training gains. Improper form may make an exercise easier to do (by cheating) but it will not bring the gains you expect. Fewer repetitions done correctly always return better results than many repetitions done poorly.

5. *Arrange a circuit:*

When organizing your training plan, it is important not to put two exercises in a row that work the same muscles. For example, you might arrange a circuit that has one exercise each for: abs, back, chest, shoulders, legs, neck, arms, and wrists in that order. Begin with the most intensive exercises first and work toward the exercises that are easiest or that work smaller muscles groups. Limit the number of exercises to no more than ten different types at each workout. If you plan to do more than one set of each exercise, run through the whole circuit once and then go back and do a second run through so you have done two sets of each exercise. By doing the exercises in a circuit format rather than doing one set, resting and doing a second set, you will save a tremendous amount of time while still giving each group of muscles a break between sets.

Power Exercises

*You may vary the height, intensity and frequency of the following exercises according to your current fitness level.

P-1 PUSH-UPS

Execution: Push-ups should be done with the hips straight and the upper and lower body aligned. Bend your elbows to ninety degrees when you lower your body and straighten them fully when you raise it. Push-ups may be done with the palms flat or on the knuckles.

Fitness benefits: Strengthens the chest, arms, shoulders and wrists.

Martial arts benefits: Improves strength in upper body striking and weapons skills.

P-2 Fist clench

Execution: Grasp a small, firm ball in the fist and squeeze tightly then relax.

Fitness benefits: Strengthens the hand and arm.

Martial arts benefits: Improves grip strength.

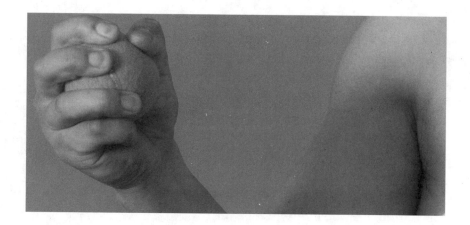

P-3   STICK TWIST

Execution: Grasp a stick or staff in the middle. Rotate your hand and forearm to the left and right alternately while keeping your upper arm stationary.

Fitness benefits: Strengthens the hand wrist and forearm.

Martial arts benefits: Improves grip strength.

P-4 HANGING LEG RAISES

Execution: Hanging from a chin-up bar, raise your knees to your chest.

Fitness benefits: Strengthens the abdomen, chest and shoulders.

Martial arts benefits: Improves upper body and torso strength for throwing, kicking and striking.

P-5   CURL-UPS

Execution: Lie on your back with your knees bent and your feet flat on the floor. Place your hands on your chest and raise your chest slowly until your shoulder blades are off the floor. Hold for five seconds and relax. If you have back pain, lie back and raise your knees off the floor. Keeping your lower back on the floor, raise your shoulders up towards your knees, hold for five seconds and relax.

Fitness benefits: Strengthens the abdomen.

Martial arts benefits: Improves upper body and lower body coordination by strengthen the connective muscles in the torso.

P-6 BACK EXTENSIONS

Execution: Lie on your stomach with your hands clasped behind your head. Raise your upper body off the floor, hold five seconds then lower it.

Fitness benefits: Strengthens the back muscles.

Martial arts benefits: Strong back muscles support the trunk in all martial arts movements.

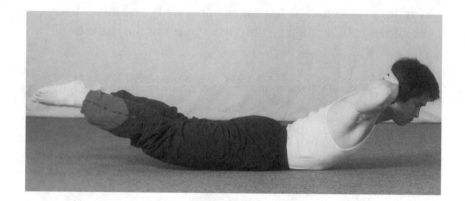

P-7 SIDE LEG RAISES

Execution: Lie on your side with your legs extended. Lift your top leg toward the ceiling and then lower it. For an added challenge, wear two or three pound ankle weights.

Fitness benefits: Strengthens the trunk and leg muscles.

Martial arts benefits: Improves kicking and stance strength.

P-8 LEG SCISSORS

Execution: Sit with your hands behind you for support and your legs extended in front of you. Lift both legs off the floor and cross and uncross them sideways in a scissors motion. Then switch and move them up and down in a similar motion.

Fitness benefits: Strengthens the abdomen and leg muscles.

Martial arts benefits: Improves leg and trunk strength for kicking, throwing and grappling.

P-9 LUNGES

Execution: Stand with both feet shoulder width apart. Step forward into a deep stance and then return to the starting position. For an added challenge, hold a barbell over your shoulders.

Fitness benefits: Strengthens the legs.

Martial arts benefits: Improves leg strength for deep stances, grappling, throwing, footwork and kicking.

Cautions: If you have knee pain, bend less deeply and lighten the load. If the pain continues, stop this exercise.

P-10 Squats

Execution: Stand with both feet shoulder width apart. Slowly lower your body and flex your knees then stand up. For an added challenge, hold a barbell over your shoulders or squeeze a soccer ball between your knees.

Fitness benefits: Strengthens the legs.

Martial arts benefits: Improves leg strength for deep stances, grappling, throwing, footwork and kicking.

Cautions: If you have knee pain, do not bend more than ninety degrees and lean against a wall to support your back as you squat.

P-11 CALF RAISES

Execution: Stand with both feet shoulder width apart and raise up onto your toes. Hold for a ten count and lower. For an added challenge, hold a barbell over your shoulders.

Fitness benefits: Strengthens the calves, feet and ankles.

Martial arts benefits: Improves leg strength for deep stances and footwork.

1. Strength training can be isometric or isotonic. Isotonic exercise is good for rehabilitating joint injuries while isometric results in measurable gains for martial arts training.

2. Rip cord training is highly beneficial for developing power in specific martial arts skills

3. Weight training is a good supplement to martial arts training. A program of moderate repetitions (8-12) is best to maintain flexibility and speed while increasing power.

4. Strength training should be specific to the activity that you want to improve. The more closely your strength training resembles your target activity, the faster you will see results.

5. Strength training can be done in many ways, with or without equipment.

6. Proper form is a very important part of the strength training equation. Concentrate on form first and adding weight or resistance second.

7. Do no more than ten different types of strength building exercises in one workout. Alternate routines, working one set of body parts on one and another set the next day.

8. By working in a circuit routine, you can minimize wasted time and gain aerobic benefits.

chapter 9

Reflexes after 40

Martial arts training is a great way to keep your reflexes sharp. As you grow older, the communication speed between your mind and your body begins to slow and this has a direct impact on your reflexes. You may first notice this change in sparring. Where you used to be able to quickly side step and counter an attack with speed and accuracy, you may now be feeling a bit slower. You may be a step behind your younger classmates where before you were a step ahead.

One of the best ways to sharpen your reflexes is to keep using them. Include drills that sharpen reaction time, such as the ones described in this section, in your training, . In addition to your martial arts training, regularly engage in hobbies or recreation activities that require quick reactions such as video games, ping-pong, or playing along with Jeopardy at home.

SPARRING REFLEXES

Many novice and intermediate martial arts students find that their most noticeable area of weakness in reflexes is during free sparring. The ability to react to the many variables in sparring is a learned skill, one which requires a great deal of practice to master. If you are a beginner at sparring or if you have a great deal of difficulty with your reaction time, you will benefit from structured practice with a cooperative partner.

ARRANGED SPARRING PRACTICE

Begin with a very basic technique, like a straight punch. Determine what your reaction will be (block, sidestep, duck, etc.). Try to keep it very simple at this point so you experience success from the start. Begin the exercise with you and your partner moving around naturally as you would in sparring. Your partner may throw the predetermined skill at any time and you should react as quickly as possible with your predetermined response. Stick to just one attack and one response until you can effectively respond to your partner every time.

When you feel confident with one response, add another. You may choose between blocking or ducking. Or you may have your partner add a second skill, using a left hand punch sometimes and a right hand punch other times. If your partner is alternating skills, then you should be alternating responses as well. When you can effectively work with two skills, add another. Keep adding variety as you increase your skill and confidence level.

LIMITED FREE SPARRING

After a while, the structured nature of this drill will become too easy. This is the time to move to the next level, which is limited free sparring. Before you begin, decide what skill you will use for attacking. Pick only one basic skill that both you and your partner can randomly attack with, such as straight punch or front kick. In limited sparring, either person can attack with the chosen skill at any time and the other person must respond quickly with an appropriate technique. This is one step closer to free sparring, but gives you a known range of possible responses so you can be better prepared to react to each attack. You may need to return to this drill when you learn complex attacks or counters that you find difficult to apply in free sparring.

SOLO PRACTICE

If you don't have a partner who can help your practice you can use any randomly generated stimulus as a cue. For example, you could use a video tape of a sparring match and react to one of the fighter's attacks. Or use your favorite sitcom and respond to a certain cue, such as every time a character says another character's name. It is important that the cue be random and unanticipated, just like an attack in sparring. If you know that the cue is coming, you will improve your speed, but not your reflexes.

Reflex Exercises

*You may vary the height, intensity and frequency of the following exercises according to your current fitness level.

R-1 REACTION DRILL

Execution: Have a partner randomly throw various attacks at you while you try to respond quickly and correctly with a block, counter or other response.

Fitness benefits: Improves reaction time

Martial arts benefits: Improves response time in sparring and self-defense situations.

R-2 SKILL SELECTION DRILL

Execution: Using one or two hand held targets, have a partner present the targets at random intervals. Before you begin, agree on what skill will be thrown for each target position, such as straight punch for a vertical target, hook for an angled target and front kick for a low target. Try to respond with the correct skill as quickly as possible after your partner presents the target. For added difficulty, work with combination skills.

Fitness benefits: Improves reaction time

Martial arts benefits: Improves response time in sparring and self-defense situations.

R-3 HEAVY BAG WORKOUT

Execution: Let the bag swing freely and attack it at random. Do not stop the bag, but try to direct it through the use of appropriate strikes and footwork. Go with the movement of the bag.

Fitness benefits: Improves reflexes

Martial arts benefits: Improves response time and technique selection in sparring and self-defense situations.

R-4 DOUBLE END BAG WORKOUT

Execution: Strike a double ended bag or ball concentrating on continuous, rhythmic movements. Move with the bag and practice evasion as well as attacking skills.

Fitness benefits: Improves reflexes, speed

Martial arts benefits: Improves response time and speed in sparring and self-defense situations.

R-5 CHALK SPARRING

Execution: Face a partner in sparring stance. Each of you should hold a piece of colored chalk in one hand. Try to mark your partner's clothes or uniform with the chalk while avoiding getting marked by him.

Fitness benefits: Improves reaction time, speed, agility

Martial arts benefits: Improves offensive and defensive skills in sparring and self-defense situations.

THINKING POINTS

1. Martial arts training naturally improves reflexes.

2. Reflexes are best improved through activities that require a quick and un-anticipated response like sparring, playing video games, table tennis or quiz games.

3. Sparring reflexes can be best developed through a progressive program of practice beginning with limited skill practice and working up to free sparring.

4. Reflexes may need to be retrained when new, more complex skills are learned. Going to back to limited skill practice using the new skills is often helpful.

chapter 10

Coordination after 40

Our ability to improve coordination, the regulation of muscles by the nervous system, peaks in our teens. However, many martial artists find that the holistic nature of martial arts movements improves coordination unlike any other sport. Many adults have labeled themselves hopelessly uncoordinated after a childhood of sports related nightmares only to find that they can progress consistently in their martial arts training. Coordination plays a significant role in learning new skills and in improving the speed of skills once they are mastered. By working on your coordination, you will find that your overall performance improves markedly, particularly in the early stages of learning new skills.

Coordination is affected by your sense of rhythm, sense of balance, spatial awareness, and the appropriateness of your movements across a specific timeline. There are different levels of coordination. When you first learn a skill, concentrate on practicing the skill in a vacuum, without demands on speed or reaction time. When you have learned the general shape of the movement, concentrate on adding speed, but under controlled conditions, such as practice on target pads. The final stage of coordination development is to be able to perform a skill with speed under varying circumstances, such as in a sparring or self-defense situation.

STEPS TO DEVELOPING COORDINATION

In the early stages of learning a new skill, practice the rough shape of the movement rather than striving for perfection. Concentrate on the initiation movement and the gross (large muscle) motor skills required. Select one or two concentration points, such as the chamber of a kick and foot position on impact. As you practice, emphasize these two areas while disregarding other areas. When you have mastered the execution of your concentration points, add one or two more until you can make a consistently good execution of the skill.

Skills that require standing on one leg, complex skills, or jumping skills are strongly influenced by your sense of balance. You can develop balance in a technique by exaggerating the amount of time you spend standing on one leg, closing your eyes during the execution of the technique, moving slowly through the movement with a spotter, checking your center of gravity or support, and experimenting with using different parts of your body to compensate for a loss of balance.

Try watching your movements in a mirror or videotaping yourself so you can see if your body is out of alignment during a segment of the movement, causing you to lose your balance. Check to see if your arms or legs are flailing around, your head is moving too much, your torso is tipping over or your hips are sticking out too much in one direction. In most martial arts movements, body alignment is the key to balance and coordination.

The second stage of coordination development involves the addition of speed to a movement. Of course, form should not be sacrificed for speed. Gradually make the movement quicker, adding about five percent speed with each good repetition. If a repetition is poor, stay at the same speed or drop back a bit until you can create a satisfactory execution.

When you achieve full speed with a technique, the final stage of coordination can be introduced: applying the skill under varying conditions. There are many ways to practice varying conditions such as adding footwork, creating combinations, or using the skill at random in sparring. Applying skills can make you suddenly feel uncoordinated all over again. Occasionally, you may wonder what happened to that great technique you've been practicing for weeks. It seems to fly out of your mind when you need it most, leaving you tied up in knots.

COPING WITH FRUSTRATION

There may be two sources of your frustration: your spatial coordination or your synchronization of your total body movement. If you are applying a skill against a partner, you may find that you are too close or too far away or that the skill just doesn't seem to work. To improve spatial awareness for a skill, practice specific situations in slow motion with a cooperative partner. Have the partner recreate a sparring or self-defense situation moving at half speed so you can look at the exact distance and timing you need to achieve without being rushed.

If you find that your new skill seems to be falling apart under stress, your body may be out of sync. Practicing by yourself allows you to fully concentrate on a single skill without distraction. However, practicing target drills in a line with ten other students anxiously waiting behind you can throw off your movements in a flash. You may find that your hips are moving too soon, your spins are skewed, your shoulders are out of alignment or your hands are far ahead of the rest of your body. Again, you need to break down the movement and focus on one or two concentration points. Determine where the synchronization is breaking down and focus only on that area during execution. Don't worry about a perfect execution yet. It will come after you fix the major deficiencies that are cropping up under stress.

WEAPONS AND COORDINATION

Martial arts that use weapons are good for improving your coordination. When you practice with a weapon, you quickly discover the faults in your movements because the path of the weapon exaggerates each movement. Practicing with a short or long stick is a good way to increase the synchronization between your upper and lower body and to improve your eye-hand coordination. If you have never learned to use a weapon, start with the short stick (joong bong) skills in Chapter 20.

Coordination Exercises

You may vary the height, intensity and frequency of the following exercises according to your current fitness level.

C-1 ROPE JUMPING

Execution: Jump rope for periods of three minutes with a one minute rest between. Try jumping with two feet together, alternating feet, hopping on one foot and crossing your hands between jumps. Alternate methods to keep the exercise challenging.

Fitness benefits: Improves total body coordination.

Martial arts benefits: Improves rhythm and coordination for sparring and other total body activities.

C-2 SLOW KICKING

Execution: Stand on one leg and slowly execute a kick at waist level. Keep an even speed and focus on correct execution. The extension of the kick should take a minimum of ten seconds.

Fitness benefits: Improves total body coordination, strength and balance.

Martial arts benefits: Improves balance and coordination for kicking.

C-3 BICYCLING

Execution: Lie on your back and raise your hips. Move your legs as if you were riding a bicycle.

Fitness benefits: Improves total body coordination, strength and agility.

Martial arts benefits: Improves upper and lower body coordination and orientation on the ground.

C-4 HEAD STAND

Execution: Kneel and place your palms and head on the floor. Slowly raise your knees off the floor and extend your feet toward the ceiling. Once you have mastered the basic head stand, split your legs to the side or to the front/back then return to the extended position.

Fitness benefits: Improves total body coordination, balance, neck strength and agility.

Martial arts benefits: Improves balance and coordination in a spatially disoriented position such as you might encounter in grappling or being thrown.

Cautions: Falling over backward during a head stand could result in serious back or neck injuries. Use a wall or partner for support until you have mastered this exercise.

C-5 SIDE SCOOP

Execution: Jog forward and reach down with your right hand to scoop the ground on your right side. Then use your left hand on your left side. Alternate while jogging for about fifty yards.

Fitness benefits: Improves total body coordination, agility, balance, and leg strength.

Martial arts benefits: Improves ability to change heights for grappling and throwing.

C-6 SINGLE LEG STRETCH

Execution: Stand on your left leg and raise your right leg behind you. Grasp your foot with your right hand and pull it up and toward you while lowering your upper body. Hold for ten to thirty seconds.

Fitness benefits: Improves total body coordination, balance and flexibility.

Martial arts benefits: Helps you find your center of gravity and improve balance for kicking and footwork.

C-7 SLOW KICK AND HOLD

Execution: Stand on your left leg and raise your right leg in an extended kicking position (side, front, round or back kick). Hold for ten to thirty seconds. If you need help maintaining your balance, use a chair or wall for support.

Fitness benefits: Improves total body coordination, balance, strength and flexibility.

Martial arts benefits: Improves coordination, balance and strength in kicking.

THINKING POINTS

1. Martial arts is among the most beneficial sports for improving coordination because the movements are progressive and students can work at their own pace.

2. Coordination is affected by rhythm, balance, spatial awareness and the appropriateness of movements.

3. To build coordination in new skills, practice the rough shape of the movement first and concentrate on the details after you have a basic foundation built.

4. Watching yourself in the mirror or on video tape can help you spot problem areas and correct them, enhancing the coordination in movements.

5. Spatial awareness can affect your coordination when working with a partner. Walk through problem movements slowly with your partner to spot spatial problems.

6. Practice movements both alone and under stressful conditions to ensure your coordination holds up under pressure.

7. Learning to use a weapon can enhance your coordination in ways that empty-handed movements cannot.

chapter 11

Speed after 40

Martial artists use several types of speed in training: reaction speed, initiation speed and sustained speed. Reaction speed refers to how quickly you can execute a technique in response to a stimulus such as your opponent's attack or your instructor's command. It is dependent on your nervous system as well as your muscular speed. Initiation speed refers to how quickly you can execute a single skill from start to finish and is highly dependent on the efficiency of your body's anaerobic energy production system. Sustained speed refers to your ability to do a number of skills quickly in sequence or in combination. It relies on muscle speed, coordination and muscle endurance.

Speed is primarily a movement specific attribute. You may have a very fast right hand jab, but a relatively average left hand jab. Speed in one skill does not necessarily translate into speed in another skill because it depends as much on practice and technical understanding as on raw physiologic capacity. Beyond skill specific speed, some overall gains can be made through the general understanding of the principles of speed including relaxation, initiation, flexibility, explosive strength, reaction time, and mental focus. Principles, once understood can be easily translated across all martial arts skills, even across all sports you practice.

Fast Twitch and Slow Twitch Muscle Fibers

There are two types of skeletal muscle fibers, fast twitch and slow twitch. Fast twitch muscle fiber has a high capacity for anaerobic energy production. Slow twitch muscle fiber generates energy through aerobic energy production. The type of muscle fibers present can have a great impact on your body's ability to perform. The average sedentary adult male has about 45 to 50% slow twitch fibers. Successful endurance runners, on the other hand, usually have 80 to 90% slow twitch fibers in their legs, enabling to produce aerobic energy very efficiently. Unfortunately, little can be done to change the distribution of slow and fast twitch fibers in your body. Genetics largely determine the types and percentages of muscle fibers you have.

The good news is that you can improve the capacity of each type of muscle fiber with exercise. By training for aerobic or anaerobic endurance, you can improve the metabolic efficiency of the target muscle fibers, slow twitch for aerobic activities and fast twitch for anaerobic activities.

Anaerobic Conditioning

The capacity to perform explosive or intense exercise for up to ninety seconds depends primarily on anaerobic energy metabolism. If you want to improve the amount of power and speed you can generate anaerobically, such as during short intense bursts of kicking or explosive grappling, you need to train specifically for anaerobic energy production. This is best done by overloading the anaerobic energy production system for five to ten seconds at a time.

The need for this type of rapid energy metabolism is obvious in many martial arts situations. Competitors rely on explosive movements to attack and defend in sparring or grappling. Martial artists may also need to generate a sudden, explosive response in a self-defense situation or when breaking boards. While the average martial arts class primarily trains the aerobic energy production systems through relatively steady, moderate demand activities, some training time in every class should be devoted to anaerobic conditioning to develop speed and explosive power.

During the first six seconds of intense exercise, energy is produced entirely from the breakdown of stored high energy phosphates (ATP and CP). Energy is released almost immediately in these reactions and does not require oxygen. To increase the effectiveness of short duration, explosive movements, the ATP-CP energy system must be developed to its fullest. You can increase your capacity for explosive movements by practicing very short, intense bursts of activity, between five and ten seconds in duration. Include numerous bouts of brief but intense exercise interspersed with rest periods in each training session. Remember to work the specific muscles you want to develop in the way you want to use them. In other words, do the activity you want to improve.

DEVELOPING SPEED

There are some rules to keep in mind when developing speed in your skills:

1. The skill must be conducive to speed training.

Most martial arts skills can be done at full speed, either in the air, with a partner or against a target. Gross motor skills are more easily adapted for speed training than precision skills.

2. The skill must be fundamentally physically sound.

Do not try to build speed until you have mastered the basic physical model of a skill. If you have to think about the mechanics of performing a skill or you are performing it without the correct biomechanical form, your potential for speed development is limited.

3. Relax.

Speed training requires relaxation from the point of initiation right up to the point of impact. At the point of impact or maximum intensity, the muscles should briefly tense and then relax again to facilitate quick recovery.

4. Recover.

Recovery between executions is essential for improving speed. If you are training a single skill, like front kick, the recovery between kicks can be brief, up to fifteen seconds. If you are working on combinations, spend a bit more time between repetitions so you do not become fatigued too early.

5. Practice first, practice last.

There are two theories on where in your workout speed training should come. Many experts advise putting speed training early in the workout so you are not fatigued and your muscles are fresh. This is good advice if you are relatively flexible, have good muscular endurance and can relax easily. There are two drawbacks to doing speed training early in a workout: you can become too fatigued to perform well later in the workout and you may be too tense to fully achieve your potential. Practicing speed skills near the end of a workout means your muscles are looser and therefor you may find it easier to relax, although you may sacrifice some freshness. Arrange your speed training to suit your performance style.

6. Use low repetitions.

Keep the number of repetitions of each skill low (less than 10) but the quality of each repetition very high. Perform each technique with complete concentration and commitment, resting and focusing between repetitions.

7. Feel the speed.

As you perform each repetition, you may find that a particularly fast repetition "feels" different from all the others. Try to capture and recreate this feeling, whether it is a feeling of lightness, relaxation, energy, intensity or whatever name you assign to it.

8. Take time off.

As you practice for speed, you may find that you have hit a speed bump, a pace which you can consistently imitate, but cannot break through. When this happens, it's time to take a few days to a week off from speed training. Instead of practicing the technique, spend time each day visualizing breaking through the speed bump. When you return to speed practice, do so with a fresh mind and the intent to break through to a new level. Your mind must overcome your body's perceived limitations.

9. Psych up.

If you find you still cannot break through your speed bump, try psyching up through the use of music, visualization or a little friendly competition with a classmate or the stopwatch. Sometimes a little mental boost or change of scenery is all you need to break through.

PLYOMETRICS

Many martial artists advocate the use of plyometric drills for improving explosive speed. Plyometric exercises are those which require the quick reloading of muscles during contraction, such as jumping off a box, landing and immediately jumping up again. Plyometric exercises stress the rapid generation of force, primarily during the "eccentric" (stretching) phase of muscle action. This increases the muscles' ability to sustain a load throughout its range of motion, translating strength into power more efficiently.

For older martial artists, in fact for anyone other than conditioned athletes, the risks of plyometrics may outweigh the potential gains. Plyometrics place explosive strain on the joints, raising the risk for ligament and tendon damage. While plyometric exercises can be done slowly to lessen the strain on the joints, they are no longer plyometrics, but simple strength training exercises. The very nature of plyometric training requires explosive, intense movements.

If you plan to try plyometrics consult with a personal trainer or strength coach to select suitable exercises. As a rule, plyometrics should never be attempted until you can successfully handle an overload of 150% to 200% of the maximal load. For the example of jumping off a box and immediately jumping up, you should be able to squat at least 150 to 200% of your body weight (the load your legs will lift off the ground) prior to attempting the exercise. Plyometrics training sessions should be limited to no more than twice a week to allow for sufficient recovery of the muscles involved.

A sampling of common plyometric exercises are included in this chapter to give you an idea of what plyometrics are like and how their use might influence your martial arts training. Add them to your training routine only when you meet the 150% to 200% overload criteria.

PLYOMETRICS CAUTIONS:

1. Never do plyometrics on a hard surface like concrete. A surface that "gives" on impact, like a carpeted wood floor or a wrestling mat to reduce the stress of impact on your joints.

2. When using equipment to jump off of or on to, it should be firmly fixed in place and rough surfaces that provide good traction.

3. When using equipment to jump over or move around, it should be pliable so it will give in easily if you fall on it.

Speed Exercises

*You may vary the height, intensity and frequency of the following exercises according to your current fitness level.

S-1 PLYOMETRIC BOUNDING

Execution: Leap forward or side to side with long, bounding strides. Concentrate on taking off from your foot as soon as possible after it contacts the ground.

Fitness benefits: Improves speed, coordination, agility and leg strength

Martial arts benefits: Improves footwork speed and jumping/pushing strength in the legs

Cautions: Do not do this exercise if you have a pre-existing knee or ankle injury.

S-2 INITIATION DRILL

Execution: Select a simple movement that you want to execute faster. Isolate the initiation portion of the skill, such as the chamber or pivot. Practice the initiation movement only, as quickly as possible. Once you have developed a quick initiation, practice letting the rest of the movement flow from it.

Fitness benefits: Initiation speed, timing, coordination

Martial arts benefits: Increases the speed of individual skills

S-3 WHISTLE DRILL

Execution: One person performs a simple footwork drill like sliding to the right. When his partner blows a whistle or claps, he quickly changes direction, sliding to the left. Allow one to five steps between direction changes.

Fitness benefits: Improves foot speed, coordination, agility and reflexes

Martial arts benefits: Increases speed of mobility for sparring

Caution: Do not practice this drill if you have a pre-existing knee or ankle injury. Quick changes in direction place a great deal of stress on the knees and ankles.

S-4 SPRINTING

Execution: Run a distance of ten to fifty yards as quickly as possible. Walk back to the starting line and repeat five to ten times.

Fitness benefits: Improves leg speed, leg strength and endurance

Martial arts benefits: Improves speed and strength for kicking, jumping, stances, stand-up grappling and footwork

S-5 UPHILL OR STAIR RUNNING

Execution: Jog briskly up a set of stairs or a moderately steep hill. If you do not have stairs or a hill, run in sand.

Fitness benefits: Improves explosive leg speed, endurance, power

Martial arts benefits: Improves initiation speed for kicking, footwork, jumping and stand-up grappling

Cautions: Never run downhill or down stairs. Use the down hill portion of the exercise as a walking recovery period. This type of running places extraordinary stress on the heart. Only do these exercises if your heart is healthy, you exercise regularly and you are in good physical condition.

S-6 PLYOMETRIC JUMPS

Execution: Place a heavy bag or soft target on the floor. Stand next to it sideways. Jump over it, side to side, with both feet together. You can also jump forward and backward over it or line up several targets and jump over them, one by one, in a row.

Fitness benefits: Improves speed, coordination, agility and leg strength

Martial arts benefits: Improves speed and strength for jumping, kicking, stances and stand-up grappling

Cautions: Do not do this exercise if you have a pre-existing knee or ankle injury.

S-7 WATER TRAINING

Execution: In a pool or body of water where you can stand comfortably, practice executing skills you want to improve. Water training is an excellent way to rehabilitate injured joints.

Fitness benefits: Improves speed, coordination, endurance and strength

Martial arts benefits: Improves skills by providing consistent resistance throughout the entire range of motion of a skill

Cautions: Practice with adequate supervision. You must know how to swim, even when practicing in shallow water.

S-8   ELASTIC TUBING OR BAND DRILLS

Execution: Using a bicycle tube, thera band or other elastic band, fix one end to a stationary object and use the other end to provide resistance for kicking, punching or throwing skills. You may hold the tubing in your hand or attach it to your wrist or ankle or slip your foot or hand through a loop at the end.

Fitness benefits: Strength and initiation speed

Martial arts benefits: Improves speed and power in the specific movements practiced.

Cautions: Fast or jerky movements may result in joint injuries. Use an appropriate weight band or tubing for your skill and fitness level.

1. Speed in the martial arts includes reaction speed, initiation speed and sustained speed.

2. Speed is primarily movement specific. Speed in one movement does not necessarily translate to speed in all movements.

3. Training for speed should be undertaken only after a movement is fundamentally physically sound.

4. When training for speed, keep the number of repetitions of each skill under ten.

5. While you cannot change the composition of fast and slow twitch muscles, you can enhance the quality of the muscle tissue you have.

6. The generation of sudden, explosive movements is dependent on the efficiency of your anaerobic energy production system.

7. Plyometric exercises can increase speed, but there is some risk of injury involved for older martial artists. Undertake plyometric training under the supervision of a trainer or strength coach.

8. Tubing or band drills can improve speed through the use of consistent resistance through the range of motion of a skill.

chapter 12

Endurance after 40

Endurance means the ability to work continuously, without becoming fatigued. In addition to aerobic endurance, which is the ability to perform moderate work for a long period of time, there is short duration endurance (the ability to perform intensively for a brief period), muscular endurance (the ability of your muscles to perform continuously) and mental endurance (the ability to concentrate during prolonged stress). During the average martial arts class, you utilize all four types of endurance. Aerobic endurance carries you through a class successfully, short duration endurance helps you complete intensive drills at full power, muscular endurance gives you the ability to complete a set dozens of kicks or punches in a row and mental endurance allows you to learn new skills and focus during practice.

SHORT DURATION ENDURANCE

If you are training for competition or self-defense, you should be focusing on short duration endurance, preparing your body to go all out for thirty seconds to three minutes at one time, such as you might do in a round of sparring or a brief confrontation on the street. This is a form of anaerobic endurance. Unlike the anaerobic energy derived from phosphates described in the speed section, this type of anaerobic energy production relies on the reaction of glucose to lactic acid. To improve your short duration endurance, you must stress the lactic acid energy system by working at maximum output for about one minute at a time, doing the types of movements you would expect to do during an actual bout or confrontation.

Interval training is the best way to structure this type of short duration endurance training. For example, work the heavy bag with full power, nonstop combinations for thirty seconds followed by a two minute rest. (Rest periods should be filled with light activity such as walking, stretching or breathing exercises to minimize the stress on the body at the start of the next repetition.) Repeat this cycle five times, going full out during each round.

Ten minutes of interval training causes greater stress on the lactic acid energy production system than a single ten minute session of heavy bag training because after ninety seconds of sustained exercise, your aerobic energy production systems kick in and take over some of the stress from the anaerobic energy production system. The anaerobic energy system can only deliver energy for about sixty to ninety seconds of full speed activity.

Interval training or any type of intense anaerobic training should always be done at the end of a workout because it results in significant build-up of the waste product lactic acid in the muscles, which can adversely affect other areas of training. Lactic acid build-up can take a significant period of time to recover from and recovery during a training session is not possible.

AEROBIC ENDURANCE

When we think of endurance, most people think of aerobic endurance, the ability to run long distances or to work out for a sustained period of time. Aerobic energy, the energy we need for sustained periods of exercise longer than ninety seconds, is produced when oxygen is delivered to the muscles to aid in the breakdown of compounds in the body for generating energy. As long as the oxygen supply is adequate, you can continue exercising with minimal discomfort or fatigue. When the supply of oxygen is inadequate, the anaerobic energy system must take over, resulting in the production of excess lactic acid, leading to fatigue.

Your body's capacity for aerobic endurance depends on your capacity for oxygen delivery, which is controlled by the heart, lungs and vascular system. When exercise is begun, oxygen uptake by the lungs quickly increases. The body's response to exercise consists of a complex series of cardiovascular adjustments to provide active muscles with the blood supply appropriate for their metabolic needs, to dissipate the heat generated by active muscles, and to maintain the blood supply to the brain and the heart. After approximately two minutes, oxygen uptake usually remains relatively stable at each intensity level of exercise. During this steady state, heart rate, cardiac output, and blood pressure are maintained at reasonably constant levels.

Aerobic endurance is important to martial arts in the sense that you will enjoy class much more if you can get through an hour's workout without huffing and puffing through every drill. If you were sedentary prior to starting your martial arts training, you may be able to improve your aerobic capacity by as much as forty percent through consistent training. If you were moderately active, you can still improve by as much as ten to fifteen percent if you adopt a regular cardiovascular training program

There are several factors that you must take into consideration if you want to improve your aerobic capacity. The average person needs to participate in an aerobically challenging workout at least twice a week to see an improvement in aerobic capacity. If your martial arts class is vigorous enough, you may be able to count class time as your cardiovascular workout. In fact, studies have shown that cardiovascular fitness is favorably affected by two to three workouts per week, but shows little additional improvement when workouts are increased to four or more times per week.

There are two methods for improving your aerobic capacity. You can train for at least twenty minutes at a moderate level of activity, one at which you can carry on a conversation. Or you can use interval training: training intensively for three to five minutes followed by one to two minutes rest, repeated three to five times. Both continuous aerobic training and interval training will improve your aerobic capacity.

Cross Training Endurance Exercises

RUNNING

Pros: Running is an excellent means of cross training for aerobic fitness and leg strength. It is also a good workout for your hips and lower back. Running is easy to do, requires very little specialized equipment and can be done just about anywhere: at home on a treadmill, at the gym, around the neighborhood, in the woods, or in the park. If you travel frequently, a running regimen might be the easiest form of cross training to keep up. Running is also a social activity that can be done with a partner or running club for added motivation.

Cons: Running has a high risk of injury to the legs and leg joints. If you are doing long distance running (more than twenty-five miles a week) you are at a higher risk of injury than if you are running 20 miles per week or less. The good news is that you don't need to run long distances to supplement your martial arts. A few miles three days a week (on days you don't train) is a nice supplement. However, if you have pre-existing knee, ankle, hip or back injuries, running may not be the best endurance training option for you.

SWIMMING

Pros: Swimming is a great means of aerobic conditioning as well as a good method for strengthening the upper body, including the arms, shoulders, back and neck. Swimming is also a good choice if you have previous injuries that make impact activities, like running, a poor choice. Water cushions and supports the body, nullifying the effects of gravity and allowing you to do things in the water (including martial arts movements and aqua-jogging) that you might find too painful to do on land.

Cons: Swimming is limited by the availability of a pool or other suitable body of water and possibly by the weather. It also requires some degree of skill. To benefit aerobically from swimming, you must be able to do at least one or two basic strokes. On the other hand, if you want to practice your kicks in the shallow end or do some deep water jogging using a flotation vest, you may be able to get away with only knowing how to dog paddle to safety if necessary. Swimming can be boring and solitary. Unlike other activities that you can do with a friend, it's hard to keep up a conversation while swimming.

CYCLING

Pros: Cycling is another good aerobic workout that builds lower body strength with the added benefit of being easy on your joints. In fact, stationary cycling is often prescribed as rehabilitation for knee and leg injuries. Cycling can be less boring than swimming or running because you can traverse long distances cycling outdoors or watch TV while stationary cycling.

Cons: Cycling outdoors can be dangerous or fatal. Always wear a helmet and use caution when cycling on roadways. Cycling can also aggravate old knee injuries if your position on the bike is incorrect or you put too much stress on your knees while pedaling.

Rowing

Pros: Rowing on an indoor rowing machine is a great total body strengthening workout in addition to an aerobic workout. It works the legs, backs, arms and shoulders all in one session.

Cons: Rowing requires instruction in form and specialized equipment. If you have access to a rowing machine and a fitness instructor at your health club, rowing is a good choice to add variety to your aerobic cross training.

Aerobics

Pros: Aerobics, whether step, dance or aerobic kickboxing, are good total body conditioning activities as well as good cardiovascular workouts. If you are already participating in a martial art that includes kicking and punching, you may be able to easily design your own "aerobic" workout by practicing combinations of kicks and punches to music or in a rhythmic fashion for twenty to thirty minutes. You can practice throwing kicks and punches in the air or to a heavy bag for variety. You can also purchase follow-along video tapes or attend a class at a health club. Aerobics require very little space, allowing you to get a good workout in your living room or hotel room.

Cons: Aerobics can appear deceptively easy while you are working out, causing you to do too much too soon. Overdoing it may lead to short-term or nagging injuries that creep up on you. In fact, many popular aerobic kickboxing programs are poorly designed, with too much emphasis on high risk or high impact movements that can lead to hip and knee problems.

Moderate your aerobic workout so that it is challenging for your heart, but easy on your joints.

CROSS TRAINING SELECTOR

Use the chart below to help you choose a cross training activity that meets your needs.

	Running	Swimming	Cycling	Rowing	Aerobics
Special equipment needed		✕	✕	✕	
Strengthens upper body		✕		✕	✕
Strengthens lower body	✕		✕	✕	✕
Can be done anywhere	✕				✕
Instruction required		✕		✕	✕
Social activity	✕		✕		
Injury Risk	Moderate to High	Low	Indoor: Low Outdoor: Moderate	Low	Low (with correct form)
Use caution if previous injuries to:	knee, ankle, hip, back		knees	shoulders, back	hip, knees

THINKING POINTS

1. There are four types of endurance at work in martial arts training: aerobic endurance, short duration endurance, muscular endurance and mental endurance.

2. Short duration endurance can be improved by stressing the lactic acid production system for periods of up to one minute at a time. Interval training is ideal.

3. Aerobic endurance can be improved as much as forty percent through vigorous and consistent martial arts training.

4. Both interval and continuous training can be used to improve aerobic endurance.

5. Cross training is a good way to maintain your aerobic endurance and fight the boredom that aerobic exercise sometimes leads to.

chapter 13

Creating a Workout Plan

Based on the exercises in Chapters 6 through 12, this chapter will provide you with guidelines for creating a workout plan based on your skill level and goals. There are five sets of exercises grouped by the attributes they develop. Depending on your goals, you may concentrate on one or two sets of exercises or choose a selection of exercises from all five groups.

Each of the exercises listed in this chapter is categorized into three experience levels: beginner, intermediate and advanced. The beginner level is intended for those new to martial arts. The intermediate level is geared to those with one to four years of experience, or up to black belt level. The advanced level is for those who are in very good shape or have at least five years of training experience.

To find the best level for you, start with the beginner recommendations and work up to a workout plan that challenges you.

5 STEPS TO CREATING YOUR WORKOUT PLAN

1. *Make a list of your workout goals*. Include the types of improvements you would like to make (flexibility, strength, speed, etc) and the areas of the body you need to work on (arms, chest, legs, back, etc.). Based on this list, choose appropriate exercises from the workout plans that follow. When choosing exercises, consult the individual listings for the benefits of exercises you are not familiar with.

2. Start with the beginner exercises and *select the exercises and number of repetitions from each section* that are best for you. Each successive plan gives you an idea of how much to increase each exercise and which exercises to add or drop as you progress. These are general guidelines from which you should adapt your personal plan.

3. There are two ways to *organize your daily workout*. You can select a theme for the day, like endurance on Monday, Wednesday and Friday and speed training on Tuesday and Thursday. Or you can mix some of each type of exercise in every workout. If you are not certain what type of plan would work best for you, start with a mixed workout.

4. When selecting exercises, it is not necessary to include every exercise from each plan. *Eliminate any exercises that may cause or aggravate injuries*. See the cautions after exercises for more specific information.

5. As you progress, your needs may change. *Update your plan monthly*. Increase the number of sets or repetitions for exercises that are becoming too easy. Drop exercises that are no longer producing results and add more challenging exercises. Rotate exercises that have similar benefits to reduce boredom.

USING THE SAMPLE PLANS

All of the sample plans are designed according to a consistent pattern:

①	②	③	④	⑤	⑥
Exercise	Reps	Beginner	Intermediate	Advanced	#
Curl-ups	10	1	2	3	P-4

In the above example, the exercise is curl-ups. There are ten repetitions in a set. Beginners do one set of ten, intermediate students do two sets of ten (twenty) and advanced students do three sets of ten (thirty).

Column ① lists the exercise name as it is found in this book.

Column ② lists the number of repetitions in one set. Every level does the same number of repetitions in a set. You can do each set with a brief rest in between or you can do all of the sets without stopping. Sets that are timed should be done with a short recovery period between them.

Column ③ lists the number of sets a beginner should do.

Columns ④ and ⑤ list the number of sets for intermediate and advanced practitioners respectively.

Column ⑥ lists the number of the exercise found in Chapters 6 through 12.

Power Exercises

Exercise	Reps	Beginner	Intermediate	Advanced	#
Fist clench	5	2	3	5	P-2
Stick twist	10	1	2	3	P-3
Hanging leg raise	10	1	2	3	P-4
Lunges	10	1	2	3	P-9
Squats	10	1	2	3	P-10
Calf raise	10	1	2	3	P-11
Curl-up	10	1	3	5	P-5
Push-up	10	1	3	5	P-1
Back extension	10	1	2	3	P-6
Side leg raise	5	2	3	4	P-7
Leg scissors	10	1	2	3	P-8

Flexibility Exercises

Exercise	Reps	Beginner	Intermediate	Advanced	#
Neck stretch	10	1	1	1	F-1
Arm circle	10	1	1	1	F-2
Arm raise	10	1	1	1	F-3
Forearm stretch	10	1	1	1	F-4
Finger press	10	1	1	1	F-5
Side bend	10	1	1	1	F-7
Knee rotation	10	1	1	1	F-10
Toe touch	5	1	1	1	F-11
Knee raise	5	1	1	1	F-13
Groin stretch	5	0	1	1	F-12
Seated trunk twist	10	1	1	1	F-6
Back stretch	5	1	1	1	F-8
Back roll	5	1	1	1	F-9
Leg extension	5	0	1	1	F-14
Ankle rotation	10	1	1	1	F-15

Speed Exercises

Exercise	Reps	Beginner	Intermediate	Advanced	#
25 yard sprint	3	1	2	3	S-4
25 yard uphill run	3	0	1	2	S-5
25 yard bounding	3	0	1	2	S-1
Initiation drill *	5	1	2	3	S-2
Rope ladder drills	3.	1	3	5	A-9
Plyometric jumps	10	0	1	3	S-6
Elastic tubing *	10	0	1	2	S-8
Reaction drill	30 sec.	1	2	3	R-1
Skill selection drill	30 sec.	1	2	3	R-2

* Exercises with a (*) are skill based should be done the stated number of reps and sets for *each skill* practiced.

Endurance Exercises

Exercise	Reps	Beginner	Intermediate	Advanced	#
Run, swim, bike, cycle, aerobics	15 min.	1	2	3-4	
Heavy bag work	1 min.	2	5	10	R-3
Rope jumping	3 min.	1	2	3	C-1
Sparring	3 min.	1	3	5	
Stair running	1 flight	0	3	5	S-5
Interval sprinting	25 yards	2	4	6	S-4

Because endurance work can be boring, vary your activities from day to day choosing from the above exercises. Include both aerobic and anaerobic activities in your workouts.

Physical Integration Exercises

Exercise	Reps	Beginner	Intermediate	Advanced	#
25 yard zigzag run	1	2	4	6	A-2
25 yard shuttle run	1	0	2	4	A-3
25 yard side scoop	1	1	2	3	C-5
Knee to chest jump	5	0	1	2	A-1
Single leg stretch	1	2	2	2	C-6
Shoulder stand	20 sec.	1	1	1	A-6
Spinal roll	5	0	1	1	A-7
Bicycling	30 sec.	1	2	2	C-3
Rope ladder	3	1	3	5	A-9
Footwork drill	30 sec.	2	4	6	A-4
Shadow sparring	1 min.	0	3	5	A-5
Slow kicking	10	2	2	1	C-2
Slow kick and hold	10	0	1	2	C-7
Chalk sparring	1 min.	0	1	2	C-4

chapter 14

Injury Prevention
and Self-care

Adults between the ages of 30 and 59 account for a significant portion of sports-related emergency room visits, primarily because they are "weekend warriors" whose bodies are just not prepared to take the kind of punishment that sports like basketball, racquetball and even martial arts can dish out. The good news is you don't have to be one of the walking wounded. With a well thought out training plan, you can prevent most injuries and enjoy martial arts for as long as you continue to train.

ELEMENTS OF AN INJURY PREVENTION PROGRAM

If you are just beginning martial arts or changing arts, you should have a complete physical exam. Be sure to speak with your physician about any past sports injuries or other pre-existing conditions that you have and how they might affect your participation in martial arts.

Once you have been cleared by a physician to begin training, your choice of an art and school are an important dimension of injury prevention. Arts that emphasize a great deal of full contact training, jumping or high kicking, hard falling or throwing are not the best choice for a forty-five year old beginner. Classes that are over-run with little kids playing ninja turtles or filled with blood hungry kickboxing teenagers are also a poor choice. Look for an art that is well balanced and geared to adults with adults-only classes.

A BALANCED CLASS SHOULD INCLUDE:

1. Conditioning and stretching exercises in every class

2. Light or non-contact sparring and/or self-defense training

3. Individual practice of forms (prearranged movement sequences)

4. Group, partner and individual skills practice, including striking and kicking with targets or heavy bags

5. Weapons practice for higher belts in many arts

6. Meditation or quiet time in each class to allow for recovery and reflection

7. Appropriate use of safety gear during contact training

8. Warm-up and cool down for every class

AVOID SCHOOLS OR CLASSES THAT:

1. Have adults participate in classes that are primarily made up of children

2. Do not break down skills by rank or teach a progressive curriculum

3. Heavily emphasize full contact training

4. Use unsafe stretching or conditioning exercises

5. Skip the warm-up or cool down

6. Don't use protection gear for all levels of contact training

7. Push students too hard for their skill or age level

Beyond these basic guidelines, always try out a class before signing up for lessons and use your own common sense. You should fccl comfortable with the other students and the instructor. You should feel challenged but not intimidated, fearful or pushed beyond your limits. If you have any questions, be sure to speak with the head instructor before registering for classes. Ask if you can go at your own pace and if there are any requirements for rank advancement, such as mandatory competition participation, that you may find difficult to meet.

Be Consistent

Once you sign up for classes, set a regular schedule of two to four classes per week and try not to miss class. By going to class regularly, you will keep your body strong and limber, allowing you to maximize your performance. If you attend class irregularly and then try to keep up with everyone else, you are asking for an injury. If you miss a class, take the time to stretch and do some aerobic activity that day so you don't lose ground.

Warm-up

Stretch before every class. Some instructors do not include a great deal of stretching in class because they expect students to arrive early and warm-up on their own. If your instructor does not stretch at the start of class, arrive fifteen minutes early and stretch on your own. Focus especially on stretching your legs and lower back. See *Chapter 7: Flexibility* for martial arts stretches.

In addition to preparing your body, you should prepare your mind for class. Since martial arts are often contact sports, you should only participate in class when your mind is sharp and focused. If you are feeling distracted, tired, sick or angry, skip class and rest or workout on your own instead. A mental slip in sparring could result in a serious injury to you or your partner. If you find that you are frequently distracted in class, try arriving early and taking fifteen minutes to meditate quietly before class.

Supplementary Weight Training

Adding some light weight training to your weekly fitness routine can greatly benefit your martial arts training. Weight training does not mean heavy weight lifting or joining a gym to use weight machines. Martial arts training benefits most from a program of light weights at higher repetitions a couple of times a week. For weight training programs designed for specific martial arts, see the book *Weight Training for Martial Artists* by Jennifer Lawler available from Turtle Press.

Use Safety Gear

If your class involves contact, always bring the correct safety gear to class and wear it. Safety gear can't protect you if it's sitting in your equipment bag. There is a wide variety of gear available for martial arts depending on what type of art you practice. As a basic requirement, all men should wear a protective cup, even during non-contact training. Accidents happen and a stray kick to the groin during non-contact practice is always possible. Better to be safe than sorry.

Additional gear for sparring can include pads for the feet, shins, hands, forearms, chest and knees depending on the art and level of contact. Densely padded headgear and a mouthpiece should always be worn if kicking or striking to the head is allowed. If you are training with weapons, head gear with a face guard and heavily padded gloves are sometimes worn during contact drills. And if you are holding boards for someone to break, always wear eye protection.

Finally, always listen to your body and use common sense. If your intuition tells you it's time to sit down and have a rest, listen carefully. Martial arts are about comparing yourself to yourself, not to the person next to you.

SAFETY IN THE CLASSROOM

There are some simple precautions every student and instructor can take to make the training environment safer. Here is a basic checklist:

1. The training area should be free of obstacles like poles, furniture and equipment that is not in use.

2. The floors should be even and smooth. If mats are used, the joints should be taped over securely so that there are no gaps or ridge for students to trip over.

3. The floor of the training area should be appropriately padded for the art being practiced. For striking arts, the padding should be dense and not more than three quarters of an inch thick. If no mats are used, the flooring should not be concrete or tile which can cause serious injuries in the event of a fall. For throwing arts, a thicker, softer surface is appropriate. For combination arts, portable mats may be used during floor work with a firmer surface for stand up practice.

4. There should be adequate lighting and ventilation, including moderate heating and cooling during the winter and summer months.

5. If weight training equipment is available, it should be housed in a separate room.

6. Any mirrors or windows that open onto the training floor should be made of non-breakable glass.

7. A first aid kit should be readily available and well stocked.

8. There should be enough space per student so that students do not collide when practicing.

9. There should not be protrusions on the wall (hooks for hanging equipment, etc.) in the training area.

10. Students practicing with weapons should be given enough space so they won't inadvertently injure another student practicing nearby.

11. Sparring practice should always be under control, with appropriate speed and contact levels according to the participants' skill level.

12. Students holding targets or mitts should be instructed in the correct method of holding equipment before practice begins.

Basic Injury Treatment

No matter how carefully you follow your injury prevention program, accidents happen. When they do, immediate and correct care of an injury will shorten the healing time and reduce pain and swelling at the injury site. Always follow the RICE principle for injuries such as bruises, pulls and strains. RICE stands for Rest, Ice, Compression and Elevation. By applying ice immediately to an injury and continuing to apply it for fifteen minute periods three to six times a day for at least 48 hours, you will reduce the inflammation in the injured area. Inflammation leads to swelling which causes pain and limits your mobility. By heading off inflammation before it gets started, you can significantly reduce your recovery time.

In addition to applying ice, you can take ibuprofen according to the package directions to further control swelling as long as you do not have stomach problems. Talk to your doctor about what type of over the counter medication is best for you. After three to four days, you can switch from ice to heat to begin to get the mobility back in the injured area and disperse waste products that have built up at the site of the trauma. Returning to full mobility as soon as is comfortable is important in preventing the injury from becoming a chronic condition. Use moist heat, such as a warm wet towel or warm soak for about twenty minutes two to three times a day.

Rest

Ice

Compression

Elevation

Post-Injury Care

Once the injury is beginning to heal, stretch the muscles in the area of the injury to counteract the effects of your inactivity and prepare to return to training. If you are unsure what types of stretches are safe or beneficial, consult an athletic trainer or ask your doctor to recommend a physical therapist. Your goal should be to return or surpass the level of flexibility that you had prior to the injury.

Rehabilitating an injury can take anywhere from a few days to a few months or more depending on its severity and location. A simple muscle pull might only take a week to heal while a ligament tear can require surgery and months of physical therapy. Regardless of the length of your recovery, you may find yourself becoming impatient and anxious to get back to class. Sitting at home imagining the rest of the class leaving you behind is not fun. If your instructor allows it, you can sit in on class and observe. Or, if your injury permits, you can participate in some segments of class and watch others.

If you cannot get to class at all, take time at home to do stretching or rehabilitation exercises. You may also be able to ride a stationary bike, swim or exercise in the water to keep up your general fitness level. You also can use the time to read martial arts related books or watch video tapes to expand your horizons. Most importantly, don't get discouraged. Stick to your rehabilitation plan and visualize yourself back on your feet and feeling great. You'll be there in no time at all.

MASSAGE

Whether you are injured or just tired from a tough workout, massage can perk up your aching muscles and relieve tension. If you are shy about getting a sports massage or cannot spare the time or money, you can always use self-massage. The following five self-massage points are guaranteed to rejuvenate and relax:

Head: There are pressure points on the skull that can be massaged to relax the entire body. The two most important points are on the back of your head at the base of your skull. You can find them by placing your hands on the ridge at the base of your skull, just above the hollow at the top of your neck. For a simple massage, put two tennis balls in a sock and lie back on the sock so that the tennis balls are pressed against the base of your skull. Pressure on these points sends messages to the spinal cord to relax the body's large muscle groups.

Face: Gently cup your cheeks with your hands and apply light pressure to your temples with your fingers. Stay that way for a minute or two as your face muscles relax.

Jaw: With your index finger, gently press the sensitive area next to your earlobe where it attaches to your head. Press and release ten to fifteen times on each side.

Torso: Ball your fists and gently rub the area above your kidneys, the soft tissue just above your waist.

Feet: Sit on the floor take one foot in your hands. First gently apply pressure to the sole of your foot with your thumb, moving from the bottom of your arch to your big toe. Then make a fist and apply pressure to your sole, moving from your heel to your toes. Next massage each toe and the webbing between your toes using your thumb and forefinger. Then press your thumbs into the bones in the ball of your foot. Finally, take your toes in one hand and support your heel with the other as you pull your toes back toward your shin. Rotate your ankle a few times in both directions and move to the other foot. If you like, you can use lotion to soothe the skin on your feet and make the massage smoother.

CARING FOR A MINOR INJURY AT HOME

1. Apply ice to bruises, sprains and strains as soon as possible after the injury occurs.

2. Continue applying ice for fifteen minute periods three to six times a day for the first 48 hours.

3. Avoid using the injured area until pain subsides. Elevate the injured above your heart level whenever you site or lie down.

4. If possible, compress the injured area gently using an ACE type bandage or elastic support wrap for the first 48 hours.

5. Take ibuprofen according the package directions (unless you have stomach problems) to ease the pain and swelling.

6. After 48 hours, switch from ice to heat if it feels comfortable to start restoring mobility and removing waste products.

COMMON MARTIAL ARTS RELATED INJURIES

Some injuries and conditions may tend to be more common in martial artists or be aggravated by martial arts training. You may find that the same kicks and punches that felt great five years ago are starting to cause nagging aches and pains. Don't despair, it's not time to quit training, just to change your approach a bit. In fact, the best antidote to many of these problems is more activity, not less. Below is a look at the most common martial arts related conditions and injuries that affect martial artists over 40 and what you can do to prevent or relieve them.

⊕ ABRASIONS

Abrasions are superficial wounds to the other layer of the skin, such as rug burn or scrapes. Abrasions may occurring during ground work or outdoor training. Treatment is simple: clean the wound with soap and water, apply some antibiotic ointment and cover the area with an adhesive bandage or gauze. The number one concern when dealing with abrasions is to prevent infection.

⊕ ARTHRITIS

Arthritis is the leading cause of disability in people over 45. It causes painful, stiff, swollen joints and sometimes painful muscles and tendons as well. The most common type of arthritis, osteoarthritis, is often caused or aggravated by a previous athletic injury, such as the type you might suffer in martial arts, tennis or football. Repeated injuries to joint, no matter how minor, can increase your chances of getting osteoarthritis, which is the result of the cartilage in a joint deteriorating. It can also be caused by being overweight or excessive stress on the joints.

If you suffer from osteoarthritis or are beginning to feel stiffness in the morning or achiness at night in a particular joint or joints, there are steps you can take to minimize the impact this condition has on your daily life.

PREVENTING OSTEOARTHRITIS

1. If you are more than 20% overweight, weight loss will definitely help, especially if you have pain in your knees.

2. Exercise regularly and focus on building strength in the supporting muscles to lessen the strain on the affected joints.

3. Wear protective gear to avoid getting hit in sensitive joints during sparring and wear elastic supports if you find them helpful.

4. Know when to rest. Taking a day or two off to rest a swollen or irritated joint can work wonders whereas pushing too hard can set you back weeks. Don't be afraid to take a day off.

5. Watch what you eat. Many people find that a diet low in saturated fat helps soothe joint pain. Be sensitive to foods that aggravate the pain in your joints.

6. Use moist heat. Some people find that moist heat, such as a warm, wet towel, applied directly to the joint soothes pain.

Apply heat for 10 to 15 minutes and then leave it off for at least one hour before reapplying.

7. Use ice. If your joints are overworked from too much kicking or punching, apply ice or an ice pack wrapped in a light towel several times a day, using a cycle of fifteen minutes on then fifteen minutes off.

➕ ATHLETE'S FOOT

Athlete's foot is extremely common in martial artists because many schools train barefoot. Once you have it, plan to live with periodic outbreaks ranging from occasional mild itching to reddened cracked skin for the rest of your life. However, with some precautionary measures, you can keep flare-ups to a minimum.

CONTROLLING ATHLETE'S FOOT OUTBREAKS

1. Dry your feet well, especially after showering or swimming. If you are still having stubborn outbreaks, try using a blow dryer at a low setting to dry between your toes after showering.

2. Fight sweat. After you take off sweaty socks, use a towel or your sock to try your feet, especially between your toes. If your feet sweat heavily, apply some roll-on antiperspirant to the bottoms of your feet before putting your socks on.

3. Stay cool. Wear shoes and socks that breath and take them off whenever possible to keep your feet cool and dry.

4. Use baking soda to absorb moisture in your shoes. It works as well as commercially prepared remedies and costs a lot less.

⊕ BACK PAIN

At least seventy percent of adults experience back pain at some point in their lives, with the first onset usually occurring sometime between 30 and 45 years of age. The problem may be a herniated disk or the beginnings of arthritis, but more likely, it will be a muscle strain. As you get older, your back muscles may get out of shape and be more likely to be easily strained by seemingly simple activities like picking up a heavy box or digging a hole in the yard to plant a tree. This type of back pain is often easily relieved without drugs or surgery. (If you have back pain that is so intense you cannot move, that spreads to your legs, if your legs or feet feel numb or tingly or if you have a fever or abdominal pain, see your doctor immediately.)

GUIDELINES FOR PREVENTING AND HEALING BACK PAIN

1. Start off the day by stretching. You can even do it while you're still in bed. First, lie on your back and raise your arms above your head. Then pull each knee to your chest slowly. Next, sit up and arch your back backwards with your hands on your lower back. Finally, slump forward and reach for your feet.

2. If you have to sit for long periods, get up and walk around at least once every hour.

3. Kneel instead of bending or squatting when working on the ground.

4. Lift with your legs. When lifting heavy objects, keep your back straight and bend your knees. Let your legs do the work.

5. Test an object before you lift it. If it's too heavy, get help rather than trying to be tough and hurting yourself.

6. Use ice for injuries. If back pain flares up, apply an ice pack wrapped in a light towel for ten minutes each hour as needed for the first 48 hours.

7. Use heat. 48 hours after an injury, you can begin applying heat to your back to increase the circulation, relax the muscles and increase mobility. Apply a warm towel for 5 to 10 minutes of every hour or take a hot shower or bath.

8. Strengthen your back with these exercises:

a. Lie on your back with your knees bent and your feet flat on the floor. Slowly raise your shoulders off the floor toward your knees with your arms reaching out in front of you. Hold for a count of ten. Repeat five times.

b. Lie on your stomach. Tense the muscles in your right leg and raise it about six inches off the floor. Hold for five seconds and repeat five times for each leg.

c. Lie on your back and raise one leg up until it's perpendicular to the floor. Hold it for a count of ten and repeat five times for each leg.

d. Stand with your back against a wall and your feet shoulder width apart. Slide down the wall to a "sitting" position, but do not bend your knees more than ninety degrees. Hold for five seconds and return to a standing position. Repeat five times.

e. Lie on your back with your knees bent and your feet on the floor. Pull your knees to your chest without straightening your legs. Repeat five times.

f. Lie on your stomach with your hands flat on the floor near your shoulders. Push the upper part of your body upward while keeping your pelvis on the floor. Hold for a few seconds and repeat ten times.

g. Stand with your feet slightly apart. Place your hands on the small of your back and bend gently backwards. Hold for a few seconds and repeat five times.

✚ BLISTERS

If you are new to martial arts or if you train barefoot on an unfamiliar surface such as carpeting or hard wood for the first time, you may discover yourself suffering from blisters on your feet. Blisters result from friction and pressure on skin that is not yet conditioned. Correct care of a blister is important to prevent infection, especially since the blister may have been exposed during barefoot training.

TREATING BLISTERS

As soon as you notice a blister appearing, clean it with soap and warm water and apply an adhesive bandage. If the blister had broken open and there is still a flap of skin remaining, wash and dry the area thoroughly, lay the blister flap back over the exposed wound and apply an adhesive bandage. If you are going to continue your workout, cover the adhesive bandage with a wide strip of first aid tape, wrapped all the way around the foot to hold the bandage firmly in place and prevent dirt from getting in the wound. It is always best to treat blisters as soon as they appear rather than waiting until the end of the training session. If a blister becomes infected (inflamed, oozing pus), see your doctor for treatment.

BRUISES

Bruises are very common in striking arts, particularly bruises to the shins and forearms that result when bones collide during sparring. Bruises are caused by sub-cutaneous (below the skin) bleeding which occurs when a blow damages the layer of tissue between the skin and muscles. Bruises are often accompanied by varying degrees of swelling and pain.

All of the elements of a bruise (pain, swelling and discoloration) can be reduced by the immediate application of ice to the area. Ice should be applied several times a day for about 15 minutes for up to 72 hours after the injury occurs.

HEALING BRUISES

After the first 72 hours, warm compresses or warm soaks can help whisk away waste products, remove discoloration and restore movement to the area of the injury. Some people find that alternating warm compresses with an ice pack can speed the healing of bruises after the first 72 hours. Begin by applying a warm compress to the area for two minutes. Follow this with the application of an ice pack for two minutes. Alternate applications of heat and ice for ten to fifteen minutes, always finishing with a two minute application of ice. This treatment creates a pumping action, alternately opening (with heat) and closing (with ice) blood vessels to pump waste products away from the injury site.

If you experience a bad bruise, if you bruise easily, or if you repeatedly bruise a specific area such as your shin, you should consider using padding or extra padding in that area during sparring or any training that may involve contact.

Bursitis and Tendonitis

Bursitis and tendonitis are brought on by the sudden vigorous use of an out of shape joint or a sudden increase in use of a healthy joint. Often going hand in hand, tendonitis and bursitis are most likely to show up in people over 40 who have not made a point of maintaining their flexibility. Without regular stretching, muscles and tendons get tighter and rub together more, increasing the risk of inflammation and leading to bursitis or tendonitis.

Shoulders, hips, knees, elbows, and ankles are especially vulnerable to bursitis and tendonitis. Men are more likely to experience shoulder problems while women are more likely to experience hip problems. In addition to these gender based tendencies, the martial art you practice may influence the health of your joints if you do not stretch and strengthen them correctly. For example, a great deal of kicking without stretching your hips and strengthening your hamstrings and quadriceps could lead to hip or knee pain.

Preventing Tendonitis and Bursitis

1. Stretch first. Always start your workout by stretching the joints and muscles you use most. Take time to fully stretch each area and hold the stretch for about ten seconds without bouncing. When you are stretching before an activity, avoid dynamic or high speed stretches because they put your ligaments at risk. Instead focus on two to three repetitions of gentle but firm stretches held for twenty to thirty seconds to loosen up. Stretching for flexibility gains should be done later in your workout after you have broken into a light sweat by doing some aerobic activity.

2. Start slowly. Approach new movements cautiously and limit the number of repetitions you do during the first session to see how your body reacts. While your knees might feel fine when you first try out that new jumping kick, 50 repetitions may leave you limping the next day. Try a few repetitions and if you feel okay after 24 hours, add more repetitions at your next workout.

3. Work smart. If you have to make repetitive movements at work, this may create joint pain that affects or is worsened by your martial arts training. Pay special attention to stretching and strengthening joints and muscles that you use everyday on the job.

4. Kneel on soft surfaces. If you spend a great deal of time kneeling, use knee pads or kneel on a cushion to prevent bursitis of the knee. If you participate in a grappling art, wear soft, flexible cloth knee pads while training.

5. Use ice massage. Fill a paper cup with water and freeze it before your workout. When you return home, peel the cup down so the ice is exposed and rub the ice over the affected joint for two to five minutes to relieve inflammation. Do not use ice directly on your skin for more than five minutes at a time.

6. Stay warm. Keep painful joints warm at night and you are less likely to wake up stiff and sore.

7. Use aspirin or ibuprofen. Aspirin and ibuprofen block swelling, acetaminophen does not.

8. See your doctor. If you are not getting relief with exercise and self-care, see your doctor. He or she may be able to prescribe stronger anti-inflammatories or physical therapy to get you on the road to recovery.

⊕ Elbow Injuries

Elbow injuries can result from overuse, such as too much hard punching, or from falling on or being struck on the elbow. Most bruises and simple sprains can be treated according to the RICE guidelines. Occasionally, an elbow bruise may result in bursitis, which is characterized by severe swelling and tenderness for a prolonged period of time. If you suspect you may have bursitis and the symptoms are not relieved by home care (ice, an elastic support, rest), consult your physician.

⊕ Foot Pain

As you grow older, your feet begin to lengthen and flatten from wear and tear. This lack of support can be especially important for martial artists who practice barefoot.

Preventing foot pain

1. Try wearing more supportive shoes during the day and during sports activities, including martial arts if possible.

2. If you are experiencing heel pain, stretch your Achilles tendon daily by standing about three feet from a wall and stepping one foot forward to lean against the wall. Keep your back leg straight and your foot flat on the floor so you feel a gentle stretch in the back of your calf.

3. Massage your foot. Roll the bottom of your foot over an unopened soup can, golf ball or rolling pin. This type of massage loosens the ligaments in the foot to ease the pain.

4. Use heat in the morning. If you have foot pain when you awaken, apply a warm compress to the bottom of your foot in the morning.

5. Use ice at night. Use an ice pack wrapped in a towel on the top of our feet at night to reduce irritation. Apply the ice for 15 minutes then take it off for 15 minutes as needed.

 ### Hamstring/Groin Muscle Injury

Injuries to the hamstring or groin muscles in the back and inside of the thigh commonly occur when activity, especially kicking, is begun without a complete warm-up. Strains of these muscles are characterized by pain or tightness in the injured muscle which often worsens with continued use. Treatment according the RICE guidelines can help speed recovery. After the initial pain lessens, daily stretching and a thorough warm-up before every workout can prevent re-injury.

Hand Injuries

Hand injuries, particularly bruises to the knuckles and jammed fingers, are common in striking arts. Mild bruising and swelling should be treated according to the RICE guidelines. If you return to training before a finger injury is fully healed, you may find it helpful to tape the finger for added support. If you suspect you may have a fracture or serious sprain, characterized by severe swelling of the injured area or decreased movement of the joint, consult your physician.

⊕ Head Injuries

If you experience a blow to the head that results in unconsciousness, no matter how brief, you should be examined by a physician. If you are struck in the head and experience nausea, confusion, ringing in your ears, dizziness or a severe headache, you should also consult your physician. Head injuries can be potentially fatal and should not be taken lightly. After a head injury, avoid all contact activities for at least 60 days to prevent an occurrence of second impact syndrome, the potentially fatal consequences of suffering a second head injury before a prior one has healed completely.

⊕ Knee injuries

Knee injuries are very common in martial arts that involve kicking or grappling, both of which can over-stress or overuse the knees. There are four common types of knee injuries: bruises resulting from a blow to the knee, strains, sprains and cartilage damage. Sprains, strains and cartilage damage are often the result of twisting the knee while it is bearing weight, overloading the joint suddenly or overusing the joint without first strengthening the hamstring and quadriceps muscles. Mild knee injuries should be treated according to the RICE guidelines.

More severe injuries, characterized by severe or persistent swelling, lingering pain, occasionally "locking out" of the joint and/or decreased stability or range of motion should be assessed by a physician before you return to training. Recurrences of mild knee injuries can be prevented by strengthening the quadriceps and hamstring muscles in the thighs and by avoiding techniques that have the potential to overload or overextend the knees. Serious knee injuries may require surgical repair if you want to return to full strength martial arts training.

✚ Shin Splints

Although most common in runners, shin splints occasionally occur after vigorous, prolonged martial arts practice. Shin splints are characterized by pain in the front of your lower leg (shin) when you run or jump. Because they are caused by the stress of exercise, they are best relieved through rest. Avoid running, jumping and bouncing until the pain subsides. In the mean time, focus on stretching and strengthening the calf and shin muscles so they are better prepared to handle the stress of your training regimen when you return to it.

✚ Shoulder Injuries

Shoulder injuries are common in grappling arts like judo and jujitsu. The shoulder is at particular risk in any technique in which a student is thrown and lands on his shoulder or when a throwing technique is initiated by grabbing the arm and using it as a lever to throw the rest of the body. In striking arts, overuse of the shoulder, such as repeated hard punches over a period of time, can result in bursitis or tendonitis of the shoulder. In beginning martial artists, strains or sprains of the shoulder may result from sudden, forceful movements without proper conditioning of the joint.

Mild sprains, strains and tendonitis can be treated according to the RICE guidelines. Resting the affected area and using a sling or support can speed healing. As the pain begins to subside, the area should be stretched and strengthened to prevent future injuries.

⊕ STRAINS

A strain is an injury to the area where muscles and tendons connect. It is caused by a sudden forceful overloading or overuse of a muscle/tendon group. Strains can range from mild (tearing of muscle fibers) to severe (a complete rupture of the tendon) which results in loss of use of the muscle group. In martial arts training, most strains are mild, resulting in stiffness, swelling or pain in the muscle for a few days to a few weeks.

Mild strains are characterized by pain in the area during or after a movement. This is usually followed by tenderness in the area and sometimes swelling or stiffness later on. If you experience a mild strain, treat the area according to the RICE guidelines. During your recovery, avoid sudden, forceful movements involving the injured area and lightly stretch every day to maintain or restore your flexibility. Severe strains, while less common in recreational martial arts, are very serious and should be treated by a physician.

⊕ SPRAINS

A sprain is an injury to a ligament, which binds one bone to another. Like strains, sprains range from mild (stretching or slight tearing of the ligament) to severe (a complete rupture of the ligament), caused by a sudden overload or stress on the joint. Knee and ankle sprains are most common in stand up arts, while shoulder and knee sprains are most common in grappling arts. Mild to moderate sprains can be treated according to the RICE guidelines. After the initial swelling is reduced, an elastic or neoprene support can be worn during training for added stability and a strengthening of the corresponding muscles should be undertaken to support the affected joint. Severe sprains, in which the ligament ruptures, most often require surgical repair to restabilize the joint if you want to continue martial arts training.

⊕ TOE INJURIES

Injuries to the toes are very common in martial arts because most students practice barefoot. Toe injuries can result from kicking a hard surface, like your opponent's forearm or a board, or from twisting your toe on a soft mat. Treatment for most toe injuries involves applying ICE according to the RICE guidelines and taping the affected toe to a neighboring toe for support and protection during training. Avoid contact training and placing too much weight on the affected foot until the pain subsides.

OTHER COMMON HEALTH PROBLEMS AFTER 40

While the following are not martial arts related problems, they may affect your ability to participate in martial arts class. Fortunately, martial arts is also the perfect antidote to many common ills that affect us as we move through mid-life.

 FATIGUE

The problem: A general feeling of low energy, listlessness or sluggishness for days or weeks at a time can be caused by many factors including inactivity, overtraining, poor eating and sleeping habits or illness.

The solution: If your doctor has ruled out illness as the cause of your fatigue, then your body is telling you that you need to change your life-style. First look at your activity level. Are you pushing yourself too hard or are you too sedentary?

If you are burning the candle at both ends, take time to prioritize and organize your daily life. Cut out unnecessary time drains. If you are turning into a couch potato, get up and get moving. Look at your diet. Cut out foods high in sugar and fat. You may also benefit from eating more frequent but smaller meals to keep your metabolism up throughout the day and taking a multivitamin supplement daily.

⊕ HIGH BLOOD PRESSURE

The problem: Normal blood pressure is 120/80. If you are 140/90 or higher, you have high blood pressure. High blood pressure is mostly caused by stress, a low level of physical activity, obesity, sodium intake or heredity.

Solution: Moderate martial arts practice and regular exercise can significantly reduce blood pressure when it is taken along with meditation, good eating habits and breathing exercises.

⊕ SLOWING METABOLISM

The problem: Metabolism is the chemical process by which your body takes in oxygen and food and converts them to fulfill the body's growth and maintenance need or to deposit them as energy sources. It is highly active during childhood and slows down as you get older.

There are two types of metabolism: anabolism and catabolism. Anabolism is the process of taking in foods and combining them to form complex substances to use for the body's needs, or to store them as fat. Catabolism is the chemical process within the body that converts the stored fat into usable energy. An active metabolism keeps your body functioning efficiently. An efficient metabolism increases your productivity and the ability to store energy that is to be used in coping with stress of everyday life. A reduced metabolism leads to weight gain, sluggishness and an overall feeling of growing old.

The solution: Elevate your metabolism on a regular basis through movement. Keep your metabolism working efficiently on the process of energy-generation. When you are active, you have more energy and can manage daily stress more effectively.

⊕ STRESS/TENSION

The problem: Stress is unavoidable. It can be either negative or positive. It becomes a problem only when you cannot cope with it. When you are unable to respond to an external stressor, it becomes detrimental to your well-being. Common causes of unmanageable stress are the inability to fight or flee, the inability to resolve problems, overworking, unreasonable deadlines, emotional exhaustion, or guilt.

The solution: Relaxation, breathing exercises, martial arts training and sparring activities can help you reduce tension caused by stress.

⊕ WEIGHT GAIN

The problem: As you grow older, your metabolism slows down and often you become less active as work and family place more demands on your time.

The solution: Make it a point to find the time to exercise and resolve to improve your eating habits. Balance your food intake with your activity level to prevent excess weight gain.

1. Many martial arts injuries are preventable. Following safety rules and using common sense in class are the best line of defense against injuries.

2. Always consult your physician before beginning a new exercise program.

3. Take pre-existing injuries and medical conditions into consideration in your daily training.

4. Be consistent in training so your body is well prepared for the demands of class.

5. Take time to physically and mentally prepare yourself before each workout or class. Do not rely on your instructor to warm-up the class.

6. Purchase and use appropriate safety gear.

7. Treat minor injuries correctly and take enough time for healing so minor ailments do not become major or chronic.

8. Listen to your body and practice active self care.

9. Use the RICE protocol to treat injuries at home.

10. If you suspect you have a serious injury or you have a minor injury that does not improve with home treatment, see your physician.

chapter 15

Overtraining

While all athletes are vulnerable to overtraining or burning out, older athletes can fall into this trap especially easily. As an older martial artist training with younger and more athletic classmates, you may feel the need to train harder and more often just to keep up. In trying to turn back time or beat your biological clock, you may end up pushing yourself too hard, in the end taking two steps backward for every one you take forward.

SIGNS OF BURNOUT

The most obvious sign of overtraining is that martial arts is no longer fun. If you feel like you have to push yourself to go to class or training has become like work, you are probably suffering from burnout due to overtraining. Overtraining is not just the result of how much time you spend on martial arts. It can result from too much training without adequate rest between workouts, frequent high pressure performances (like competition or demonstrations), or conflicts between your exercise schedule and your personal or work schedule causing you to "burn the candle at both ends" to fit in your training. Feelings of burnout can be exacerbated by poor eating habits, lack of adequate sleep, illness, drug or alcohol use, smoking, training beyond your ability or fitness level, poor organization of your training schedule/plan and psychological stress during class.

Burnout progresses through several increasingly stressful stages. Initially, you may find that you have reached a plateau. No matter how hard you work or how much additional time you spend at training, you are not making the same visible gains you made in the past. You may be suffering from aches and pains that don't seem to have a specific cause, you may find that you legs feel like lead during class or you just can't keep up the same pace as you previously could.

The next stage is characterized by an actual decrease in performance. You may find that you are suffering from a nagging injury that hampers your ability to participate fully in class. Or you may feel discouraged as your peers progress ahead of you, leaving you feeling suddenly awkward, uncoordinated and out of shape. Or you may find that you are distracted during class, paying more attention to what you are not doing than what you are doing.

These negative feelings lead to the final stage of burnout—a complete loss of interest in training. At the end stage of overtraining, you may find that you have lost your will to train, your confidence in your abilities, and that your displeasure with your physical state is spilling over into other areas of your life, such as work or family. You may even suffer from high anxiety levels, headaches, irritability and restlessness. Hopefully, with the help of this book and your instructor's guidance, you will never have to suffer the latter stages of burnout.

How to Prevent Burnout

The number one key to preventing or stopping the progression of burnout is to recognize the symptoms early. As soon as you begin to feel the need to force yourself to go to class on a regular basis, you need to take a step back and gain perspective. Of course, this feeling should be differentiated from the average bad day when you occasionally feel too tired, too stressed or too busy to go to class. If you find it a chore to get to class more than a couple of times a month or if you frequently find yourself making alternative plans on class night, you may be beginning to burn out.

The first step to take if you suspect you may be overdoing it, is to talk to your instructor. He or she has surely experienced or seen the same symptoms over the years and may have some wisdom to share with you. Discuss the possibility of cutting back your class schedule or taking a couple of weeks off to rest and recover your desire to train. If you are teaching in addition to training, consider taking time off from one or the other for a short time.

The next step is to find physical activities that interest you outside the martial arts. Consider taking up walking, jogging, biking, hiking, rock climbing, roller blading or swimming, not as a way to supplement your training (which will just seem like more work) but as a way to relax and enjoy yourself. Find a partner to enjoy your new hobbies with so they become a social event rather than more training.

Explore other facets of the martial arts. Try reading books on martial arts philosophy or the spiritual side of the arts. Spend time each day to meditate or visualize your practice. Expand your horizons beyond the physical pursuit of mastery into a more balanced practice of mind and body unity.

Have fun. Martial arts practice shouldn't be all work and no play. You should find the opportunity to smile in class and to enjoy the social atmosphere of training with others. This doesn't mean class has to be a party, but it shouldn't be a living hell either. If you are not enjoying your training, you may want to visit other schools and compare the atmosphere to your school. Martial arts class should have a humanistic side as well as a martial side. It should uplift your soul as it hones your body.

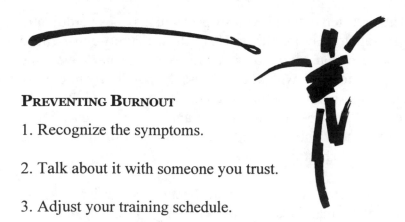

PREVENTING BURNOUT

1. Recognize the symptoms.

2. Talk about it with someone you trust.

3. Adjust your training schedule.

4. Find new activities that you enjoy.

5. Diversify your interests beyond physical practice.

6. Enjoy your training. Have fun.

THINKING POINTS

1. Older martial artists may be more susceptible to burnout as they try to keep up with younger classmates.

2. The first sign of overtraining is that martial arts is no longer enjoyable.

3. Overtraining can lead to a decline in performance and training-related injuries.

4. The key to preventing burnout is recognizing the symptoms early.

5. Combat burnout through cross training or cutting back on the amount of martial arts practice as a percentage of your overall exercise program.

Book III

YOUR MARTIAL ARTS JOURNEY

Skill Development

Traditionally martial arts have been used not only for combat and self-defense but also as a way of attaining and regaining health and fitness. Martial arts practice helps you loosen muscles and joints. It enhances your posture, balance, sense of centeredness, mobility, flexibility, power, coordination, and endurance. It also conditions internal organs, strengthens the respiratory system, and stimulates circulation. Many martial artists experience the effect of quieting the mind and achieving a sense of accomplishment as well.

Beyond all these practical advantages of martial arts training, the ultimate purpose is the attainment of physical, mental and emotional harmony.

The first step to mastery is to make efforts to move effortlessly. You need to sense yourself from inside before you begin to checking your form on the outside. In this state of body awareness, your action takes place by itself spontaneously, as an arrow shoots itself when you release it.

It is easy to say what it is like to be at the mastery level. The reality is that it takes many years to accomplish it. So you shouldn't be in a hurry. There is a saying, "The more you

It is easy to say what it is like to be at the mastery level. The reality is that it takes many years to accomplish it. So you shouldn't be in a hurry. There is a saying, "The more you hurry, the later you'll get there." You should develop exquisite physical control and equilibrium through patient, focused, and disciplined practice.

LEARNING NEW SKILLS

For most Westerners, martial arts skills are quite foreign in nature. Students who have done some wrestling, boxing or fencing find skills and concepts in martial arts that are familiar. Others may find that learning martial arts skills is like learning a foreign language. Understanding the structure of the learning process can give you an added edge in learning new skills.

There are four basic stages to learning a new skill:

STAGE 1: FORM A MENTAL IMAGE

Before you attempt to practice a new skill, you must know what the skill looks like. You may find out about a new skill by seeing your instructor demonstrate it, watching a senior student, hearing it described in detail or seeing it on video tape. By visualizing the movement, your brain begins to form ideas about its execution. You learn what parts of the body are involved, whether you will be stationary or in motion, how fast the skill should be performed, what the goal of the skill is and what the shape or path of movement should look like. Forming an accurate mental image is important in the early stages of learning, where you have little or no physical feedback to guide your performance.

STAGE 2: CREATE A ROUGH APPROXIMATION

In the early stages of practice, your goal is to create a rough approximation of the gross motor (large muscle) movements of the technique. For, example, when learning front kick, you might focus on simply lifting your leg with your knee chambered, extending your leg and retracting it. You do not need to pay a lot of attention to the position or shape of your foot, your hand position, whether your standing leg is bent or straight, etc. Focusing on creating the overall shape of the movement without too much attention to detail will prevent you from developing bad habits.

Think of learning a new skill like building a house. First you lay the foundation and put up the frame. Next you build the interior walls and then you do the little things that make the house look nice like painting and decorating. If you try to paint before you put up the walls, you will waste a great deal of time and accomplish nothing. This is very obvious in house building but less so in martial arts training. Many students get stuck on a technique when they try to put the finishing touches on a skill that is fundamentally unsound.

STAGE 3: SHAPING

The shaping stage is akin to decorating the house in the previous example. In stage two of learning, you have created a stable structure on which to build your technique. In stage three, you refine the details of the technique. Using the same front kick example, stage three is the time to make sure your elbows are close to your body, your hands are up in a guard position, your standing leg is relaxed, your toes are pointed, your knee is tightly bent during the chamber, your hips are pushing into the kick, etc. During the shaping stage, feedback is very important to your progress. Good sources of feedback are your instructor, assistant instructors, black belts, your own feeling and watching yourself in a mirror or on video tape. Use feedback to refine your movements, eliminate wasted effort and correct bad habits.

Contrary to common belief, refining a movement is not about adding good points to the movement, but about stripping away the bad points. What is left when all of the faults are eliminated is the movement as it was originally intended to be.

STAGE 4: PRECISION PRACTICE

The completion of stage three is signaled by your ability to create a correct execution of the technique. You may not be able to do it right every time, but you understand what makes the skill right or wrong. When you reach this point, you should increase the intensity of your practice. Now, instead of thinking about how to shape the technique, focus on increasing the reliability of your performance. Ultimately, this precision practice stage should lead to the point where you can perform the skill correctly on cue with a high degree of reliability.

To illustrate this process, imagine a professional golfer and good weekend golfer. An accomplished weekend golfer can most likely hit the ball the same distance as a professional. The difference between the two is that the professional can do it correctly nine times out of ten and the weekend golfer can do it maybe three times out of ten. The weekend golfer is how you enter stage four and the professional golfer is how you leave stage four. In between, you may spend hours, days or years of precision practice.

STAGE 5: INTERNALIZATION

The automatic performance of a skill with little conscious thought is called internalization. An example of a skill most people have internalized is walking. When you go for a walk, you don't think to yourself, "right foot, left foot, right foot, left foot" as you walk. You just think "walk forward" and off you go without much mental effort. As you walk, your brain monitors your progress and interjects conscious directions like "step over that rock ahead."

Internalizing martial arts movements is one of the highest levels of performance, often seen in high ranking black belts and experienced competitors. Once you have internalized a skill, it may seem like it just happens. You may be practicing a form and realize you are no longer thinking about the sequence of movements, but just executing them naturally in order. You may find that you don't have to think about some responses in sparring, you just see your opponent do a technique and respond automatically. Internalization is the last step before mastery of a skill.

STAGE 6: MASTERY

Mastery is the integration of the total package. Your mind and body function as one unit in performing. The technique has been learned well enough so that you can reliably perform it every time, yet it is not so well learned that it is inflexible or cannot be adapted according to the demands of the situation. The next section will look at the components of mastery in detail.

Enhance your ability to learn by:

1. Focusing. Keep your original goal in mind and concentrate on the task at hand.

2. Emptying your mind. Accept that there are skills that you are not good at or do not understand. Resolve to open your mind to instruction.

3. Observing. Observe your performance to gauge your progress and correct errors. Observe other skilled practitioners to model their performance.

4. Practicing. Learning is just the beginning. Practice is the cement that roots a skill in your mind and body.

MASTERING SKILLS

As a martial artist, you have learned or will learn a wide variety of skills, perhaps more individual skills than in any other physical pursuit in which you engage. Beyond just accumulating skills, your instructor expects you to practice and improve your skills, continuously pushing yourself to higher levels of technical prowess. But how can you, as a student, evaluate the quality of your skills and the rate of your progress?

No matter what your art, there are fundamental characteristics of quality human movements. Good skills are characterized by the following:

1. SMOOTHNESS

Your movements should be smooth and well blended from start to finish. When you first begin practicing a skill, you may have to break it down into segments such as initiation, extension, retraction and the return to your original position. As you progress, the segments should flow into one another until you have a single smooth movement. Depending on the complexity of the skill, this can take anywhere from one practice session to one year or more. Try to practice in a smooth, rather than segmented, movement as early in the learning process as possible. If you can learn a new movement without segmenting it, that is ideal.

2. RHYTHM

When mastered, each movement has an internal rhythm that guides it execution. It may be a consistent, measured rhythm or an unbalanced, but purposeful rhythm. What it is not is a dull, plodding performance or a tense jerky performance. The ideal rhythm of a movement is manifested as powerful grace.

3. BALANCE

Quality skills have balance. They are neither too hard nor too soft, neither too fast nor too slow. They utilize the right and left sides of the body as well as the upper and lower body adequately, without depending too much on any one area. Although they may appear outwardly to be upper or lower body skills, they use the "unused" area of the body for reaction force or compensation during movement.

4. ACCURATE

The end product of any movement is either a hit or miss, figuratively and sometimes literally. There is no "almost" in martial arts. You either hit the target or you don't, execute the throw or you don't, reverse the lock or you don't. Almost hitting a target doesn't count at the highest levels of practice. Quality movements accomplish their goal precisely.

5. RELAXED

One of the most obvious characteristics of poor movements is a tense or jerky execution during which the practitioner appears to be working against himself to accomplish his goal. Good movements are so relaxed that they appear effortless, yet they accomplish their goals with stunning power and speed. In this regard, the difference between poor performances and mastery level is the difference between swinging a telephone pole and cracking a whip.

6. ENERGETIC

Martial arts skills, by their very nature, should manifest an energy that is visible and almost tangible. While it is difficult to describe, you will know if when you see it or feel it. When your movements have internal energy, you feel as if you can fly or as if you are unstoppable. This is not an arrogant feeling, but a supreme confidence in your ability to perform to the best of your potential.

7. APPLICABLE

Quality skills are applicable to real life situations. Martial arts are warrior arts by definition and the skills you learn should work when applied against a partner or opponent. While there may be some skills that you practice for aesthetic beauty, the ultimate test of most skills is their applicability under duress. This applies both to the skill and your execution of it. Many times, a practitioner finds that a skill does not work and automatically discounts the skill as useless, when in fact it was the practitioner's execution that was at fault.

8. ECONOMICAL

Mastered skills are skills without wasted motion or effort. From start to finish, there should not be a single, unnecessary muscle movement. Every step of the technique should have a purpose and should be moving toward that purpose. Wasted motion reduces the speed of skills, hinders coordination and damages endurance.

9. ADAPTABLE

High quality skills are adaptable across a wide range of situations. If you can only use or execute a skill under certain conditions, you have not yet mastered the skill. A skill that has been mastered can be performed at any time or in any situation with little forethought or preparation. Mastered skills are also easily transformed to fit changing conditions by varying the speed, style, height, duration, range, angle or rhythm of the execution.

THINKING POINTS

1. Before you practice a new skill, form an accurate mental image of the skill as a reference.

2. In the early stages of learning new skills, focus on the gross motor movements first and then hone the fine motor movements.

3. When you can create a reliable execution of the movement, intensify the quantity and quality of practice.

4. Internalization and mastery are the highest levels of martial arts performance.

5. Learning a new skill as one smooth movement is preferable to learning it in segments.

6. Mastered skills are both applicable under all conditions and adaptable to fit changing situations.

7. Mastery of a skill requires the paring down of unnecessary muscle movement toward an economical execution.

chapter 17

Progressing in Martial Arts

Whether you are just starting out in the martial arts or have been practicing for quite some time, there are times in your martial arts journey when you find the need to recommit yourself. You might be just starting out in the martial arts, making a commitment to learn an exciting new way of moving and thinking or you might have been practicing for a few months or more and find that you have reached a plateau, physically or mentally. This is a time all martial artists face, a time to recommit yourself to training harder to getting over the hill and back on the track to improvement.

Perhaps you are a long time veteran of the martial arts, teaching students of your own and reaching the great depths of knowledge open to advanced practitioners. When this time comes, you will find the need to commit yourself anew to practice of the basics in the pursuit of mastery.

As you grow in the martial arts, you will occasionally have to set new goals, recommit yourself to your training or overcome obstacles. This chapter is a guide to your journey, a road map to help you set goals, formulate a plan and stick to it. Return to this map whenever you find your decisiveness is wavering or you find yourself starting down a new path in your training.

1) MOMENT OF DECISION

Here you are facing the moment of truth—a commitment to take your martial arts training to a new level. The only way to change is to begin the first step. No matter what happens, resolve to be positive and to be in charge!

2) SET A GOAL

Now it's time to choose a specific goal, to improve the speed of your techniques, for instance. When you frame your goal, use positive words like "to improve" rather than "to reduce". Set a goal to improve your speed rather than to reduce your reaction time. Choosing positive words fills your mind with positive energy from the beginning to the end. Now you are in charge of your goal, not the other way around.

3) VISUALIZE THE END RESULT

What changes you will experience when you achieve the goal? Will you be able to defeat younger students in sparring? Will you be more admired by your classmates? Will you have more confidence? Will you be able to do a speed break? What compels you most? What motivates you to do what you want to do? See the end result of your actions clearly in your mind so you will know when you have reached your goal.

4) DEVELOP AN ACTION PLAN

Always expect to achieve your goal. Your long-term goal is undoubtedly to improve your speed while maintaining accuracy, which will in turn lead to having more power in your techniques. But how are you going to achieve that? A huge goal is overwhelming. Concentrate on reaching it through a series of short-term objectives.

Write down your choices of activities, such as bungee cord training, anaerobic conditioning, weight training, plyometrics, sprinting, etc. Your objectives depend on your present level of fitness and the availability of time to commit to your goal. If you are in good shape to begin with, your goals can be more ambitious. If you are just starting out, your goals should be smaller at first and more ambitious as you gain experience.

5) SCHEDULE THE ACTIVITY

When you are motivated to do something, do not delay getting started. Set a specific time for the activity such as thirty minutes after class on Monday and Friday. Do not schedule anything else for that period. Ask your training partner or a family member to help you keep your scheduled commitment.

6) SELECT THE PROPER PLACE

If your goal involves running, choose a place where you can enjoy the scenery and fresh air not a road that you have to fight traffic and fumes. If you do sit-ups in your living room, turn on some high energy music to pump you up. Find a place to pursue your goal that is not only convenient but that inspires you and raises your energy level.

7) PACE YOUR PROGRESSION

Avoid trying to progress too quickly. If you go too fast, you will get sore, tired, and eventually frustrated. This will hamper your enthusiasm for your goal. You need to balance your desire and activities so that they match your ability level.

When you experience consistent and steady progress you have a better chance to succeed in achieving your goal.

8) INCREASE THE INTENSITY

Once you have found a comfortable level of activity, stick with it for seven to ten days before you increase the level. It is safe to increase the intensity of activity after the initial stage by 5 to 10 percent. Avoid taking quantum leaps from level to level. A gradual rate of progression is one of the key elements to success. Start at a level that is relatively comfortable (most successful exercisers start at 50% of their maximum capacity), but difficult enough that you know you are working.

9) REGULATE FREQUENCY

In general, working on your goal every other day or three times a week is recommended. For a serious athlete, five to six days a week may be suitable, but beyond three days a week, there is no real benefit to the recreational practitioner. It would cause more harm than benefit to do seven days a week of the same routine. There is a significant chance of injury and burn out during periods of frequent, heavy training. To prevent boredom and stay in shape, combine formal practice with cross training or something that is not as demanding as your usual routine.

10) TIME FACTOR

The amount of training time is critical for success. A minimum of 15 minutes each session is needed to achieve long-term results in most areas of training. Consistently performed short training sessions can be more effective in reaching long-term goals than long workouts that you frequently miss due to boredom or cannot find time for in your busy schedule. It's better to do 15 minutes a day three days a week than one 45 minute session per week when working on goals in the areas of speed, strength, flexibility and technique.

11) Three Stages of Training

In every activity, there are three stages your body must go through: warm up, core training, and cool down.

Warm-up

The warm-up is the beginning of a workout, in which the goal is to raise your body temperature and limber up your body. It gets your body and mind ready for training and helps reduce the likelihood of injury.

Core Training

This stage includes cardiovascular exercises, strength training and the main training you choose to do.

Cool Down

This is the transitional stage from the training period to your normal resting state. Your heart rate drops down to a resting rate through this stage. Cool down exercises include breathing, stretching, walking, or meditation. It is important that you gradually slow down. Refrain from suddenly stopping activity without a cool-down period, even if your cool-down is only walking at a moderate pace for five minutes.

12) Sequence of Exercise

After warming up, begin with the exercises you want to do most. Overall, it is safest and most productive to start with smaller, slower or precision activities first. If you are working on skills that require concentration, put these at the beginning of your workout, with more physically difficult but less intellectually challenging skills at the end of the workout.

13) Design a Training Pattern

Establishing a training pattern is important to your success. Set aside a specific time and space for your activities and stick to it. Make it a part of your daily routine. Create your own method of training that is custom tailored for your need. You don't necessarily have to do things exactly as you do them in class when you practice on your own. Set a pattern that you can most enjoy and benefit from.

14) Have a Partner

Having a committed training partner helps keep you motivated and on schedule. You may need some adjustment to accommodate your partner's training level or style initially, but the effort is well worth it if it keeps both of you motivated.

15) Progress Report

If you are working on your own program, make a progress report card for yourself. Include the date, activities, frequency, number of repetitions (intensity), and the duration of your activities. If working with weights, record the weight and number of repetitions for each set. For walking, and running, record distances and time. For skill practice, keep the record of name and frequency (or duration) of practice for each technique. These records are valuable to evaluate progress.

They will also give you benchmarks to identify when you are ready to move on to the next level.

16) Choose the Right Equipment

According to the activities you choose to do, use the necessary safety equipment. For contact activities, you must have protection gear such as head gear and a groin cup for martial arts competition, or protective goggles for swimming and racket sports.

If you use resistance machines or weights, be sure to get professional advice on how to use the equipment properly. Some equipment is very sophisticated and may cause injury if not used properly.

17) Be Realistic

Training is a long and gradual process, so you should not expect too much too soon. Over time your progress will show quite honestly. Your records are important to evaluate your progress, particularly of internal improvements.

TRACKING YOUR PROGRESS

Use this work sheet to help you set and reach a goal as described in this chapter.

1. Set your goal using specific words:

My goal is to _____

2. Visualize the end results and write down what you see:

When I reach my goal I will have/be _____
_____

3. Develop an action plan. List the activities that you think will help you achieve your goal: _____
_____

4. Schedule your activities on your weekly calendar or planner. Include the time and place for each activity.

5. *Monitor your progress in a notebook or training log. Note your starting points and increase or decrease the intensity of your training weekly according your progress and how you feel.*

6. *Have a training plan and stick to it. Sequence the exercises in your plan for the maximum benefit. If you need help, consult the fitness section of this book or talk to a trainer. Don't be afraid to experiment with your training program until you find what works best for you.*

7. *Give yourself a progress report. Once a week take benchmark tests that measure time, distance, weight or some other tangible factor. Log them in your training diary to measure your progress.*

8. *Be patient. Your progress may be slower than expected. As long as you are moving forward, stick to your plan and keep working toward your goal.*

THINKING POINTS

1. Making a commitment to take martial arts or learn a new facet of the arts requires an action plan.

2. Make your goal specific and define an end point so you know when you have reached it.

3. Visualize reaching your goal as a motivating force.

4. Creating short-term objectives is a good way to make large goals less intimidating.

5. If you choose motivating times and places to pursue your goal, you are more likely to succeed.

6. Start out at a moderate pace and increase the intensity of your activity as you progress. Starting out at a vigorous pace is likely to lead to burnout.

7. Create a sound training plan that includes a warm-up and cool down at every workout and a beneficial sequence of exercises.

8. Be realistic about your goals and reward yourself when you reach a goal.

chapter 18

Self-Defense Principles

The root of all martial arts is self-protection. While you may or may not learn sparring, forms, weapons, fitness and meditation in your martial arts classes, you should definitely be learning self-protection skills. Many people take up martial arts exclusively to learn to protect themselves or to at least feel more confident in their self-defense abilities. While they often come to enjoy other facets of the arts, self-defense is the number one reason students sign-up for classes.

Depending on the style, school and instructor you choose, the self-defense skills you learn will vary. You may learn stand-up skills like kicking and punching, ground skills like grappling and wrestling or weapon skills such as the short stick or knife. Or you may learn a combination of some or all of these elements. Learning more types of skills is not necessarily superior. Learning a few skills well and understanding the overall principles of self-defense is more important.

There are a handful of principles that are central to all methods of self-defense. As you grow older, relying on principles that can give you an advantage over a stronger attacker is more useful than trying to master a wide range of complex skills. Implement the following principles in your self-defense practice to improve your efficiency and effectiveness.

DISTANCE

Distance can be a weapon in self-protection as much as your fist or a knife. If you have a great deal of distance between yourself and your opponent, your best option is to run away. If you do not have enough distance to run away or your opponent has a weapon that is preventing you from running, try to maintain as much distance between yourself and the assailant as possible.

Ideally, you should be far enough away that your assailant's longest weapon cannot reach you unless he takes at least one step toward you. If this is not possible, try to make your centerline, your head and the central targets on your body, as far from the opponent as possible by turning your body sideways and putting your hands or any available object, such as your coat, in front of you.

OPPONENT ASSESSMENT

When confronted by an assailant, it is very important to stay calm and try to assess him. Notice his size, which hand he seems to favor (right-handed or left-handed), whether he has a weapon, his mental state (angry, serious, drunk, etc.) and what he appears to want from you. If you can give the assailant something to appease him and make him go away, do so. If you cannot, and have no choice but to defend yourself, look for vulnerabilities that you might be able to exploit to create an opportunity to escape.

PRIMARY-SECONDARY RESPONSES

Every self-defense situation can be broken down into two parts: the primary response and the secondary response. The primary response is the portion of the confrontation in which you blunt or neutralize your attacker's onslaught. The secondary response is the method you use to end the confrontation. By breaking every encounter into two stages, you can remove some of the fear and confusion from an attack and rationally face the facts.

Your first goal is to halt the progress of the attack by evading, blocking, parrying or cutting it off. You don't have to completely stop the assailant's movement, you just need to create a momentary disruption to allow you to mount a counteroffensive. A primary response can take a split second or ten seconds or a minute, depending on the size of your assailant and his skill level.

After using a primary response to make time and space for a counteroffensive, launch a quick, strong secondary response such as striking the opponent or running to safety. Remember, the goal is to escape to safety, not to win over the assailant.

The primary and secondary responses can take many forms. To illustrate, let's look at some examples:

1. Your assailant rushes you for a tackle. You side step (primary response) and knee him in the stomach (secondary response).

2. Your assailant throws a wild punch at your face. You evade the punch by ducking (primary response) and come up with a strike to his groin followed by a knee to inside of his thigh (secondary response).

3. Your assailant rushes at you to grab your shirt collar. You cut his attack with a lead hand jab which accidentally thumbs him in the eye (primary response) and leave the scene while he trying to recover his vision (secondary response).

ACT NATURAL

Avoid betraying the fact that you have martial arts training early in a confrontation because this knowledge will put your assailant on guard and make him more vicious. Instead, act as natural (and confident) as possible. Stand in a relaxed stance with your hands near your chest or waist, your back straight, your shoulders relaxed and your body turned slightly to the side. Do not assume a fighting stance or make your hands into fists. Wait as long as possible before revealing that you have a strategy or training that might help you fight back. By acting natural, you can gain the element of surprise. Once you engage the assailant, however, hold back nothing. Fully commit yourself to your defense. Your sudden change from an average person to a raging tiger will momentarily shock your assailant, possibly giving you an opportunity for a counteroffensive.

VITAL TARGETS

There are certain targets on the body that are more vulnerable than others. Targets such as the nose, eyes, throat, and groin have very low pain tolerance levels. A hard strike to one of these targets will bring even the biggest assailant down quickly. While many martial artists train to strike pressure points or use complex joint locks, only highly skilled practitioners can use these skills during a high-stress assault by an aggressive assailant. Practice all of the skills available to you , but be certain you practice simple attacks and counterattacks to vital targets along with more complex skills.

ANGLED ATTACKS

The human eye is structured in such a way that most people are more comfortable defending against attacks that come from directly in front of them rather than from angular attacks. And the most difficult angle to defend against is the blind spot that is just beyond your assailant's peripheral vision. If you can attack to the side or back of the body or head, do so. The same may also be true of low attacks. Depending on how experienced your attacker is, he may not be prepared for kicks to the shins, thigh or groin. Attacking low or angular targets can give you the advantage of surprise.

BE AMBIDEXTROUS

Practice all of the skills you learn for self-defense on both sides of the body. For example, when practicing a defense against a wrist grab, have your partner randomly grab each wrist with equal frequency, alternating right and left or practicing five on the left then five on the right. Avoid falling into the trap of practicing only your better side. A large part of surviving an attack is being able to fall back on automatic reactions that you have developed as a result of practice in the classroom. If you have only practiced on your right side, you may panic and draw a blank if a left handed attacker grabs or strikes you.

RANGE

Once you have engaged an opponent with no hope of escape, try to stay as close to him as possible. Staying close takes away your opponent's long range weapons and makes it difficult for him to generate power. It also conceals many of the potential targets on your body.

You can test the effectiveness of this strategy with a training partner. First, stand about two steps from your partner and ask him to attack you however he choose (without excessive contact). As he advances, move backward, trying to maintain the same distance between the two of you. Notice how often and to what targets he is able to attack. Notice, also, the amount of space he has to chamber and throw his attacks.

After a minute or two of observation, step forward and close the distance so you are clinching or very close to your partner. Now what types of techniques can he use? Is he able to advance and strike you repeatedly like before? Can you hit him back? Can you protect most of your vital targets? Is your partner surprised or frustrated? Done properly, the use of range should help level the playing field in a desperate situation.

Avoid Overextending Yourself

In a street confrontation, you may find that you are anxious to engage your assailant and get it over with. Resist the urge to strike first, to reach out, lean forward, throw a wild punch or in any way extend your body beyond your center of gravity. This type of movement makes it very easy for your assailant to grab you and take your balance away, possibly knocking you to the ground. Instead, wait for your assailant to come to you if he intends to. Until he moves into your space (where you can comfortably defend or counter), do not move. Just your refusal to make the first move may cause a weak assailant to back off. Even if the assailant has no intention of backing off, your refusal to be baited into making the first move will make him doubt his choice of you as a victim.

Forget the Rules

In self-defense, there are no rules. There is no sense of fair play or sportsmanship as there is in a sport-style martial arts contest. When you are attacked by an assailant, anything is fair if it helps you survive. Don't worry about what people will say later. Don't be embarrassed to run away or to fight dirty. Your assailant has no concern for being fair to you and you should not be bound by cultural training like "if I run away, everyone will think I'm a coward" or "it's not ladylike to gouge his eyes" or "my martial art doesn't believe in kicking" or "what will my buddies think if I don't beat him up?" Don't be bound by the style you practice or your gender or what skills you have learned or not learned in class. Forget everything except that you have to take every available opportunity to safely survive the confrontation.

THINKING POINTS

1. Self-protection is the essence of martial arts.

2. The self-defense skills you learn will vary according to your instructor and the style you study.

3. There are key self-defense principles that apply across all techniques.

4. Choose a limited number of skills you can do well and rely on under stress.

5. Avoid committing yourself to a line of defense until you absolutely have to.

6. Practice skills on both sides, right and left, to avoid being caught off-guard.

7. There are no rules in self-defense. Use any available tactic, skill or weapon to end the confrontation and escape safely.

chapter 19

Sparring

Martial artists engage in free sparring as a test of skills under an accepted set of rules. Sparring may involve kicking, punching, knee strikes, grappling or weapon skills. The contestants may wear safety gear such as head protection or a groin cup, depending on the amount of contact allowed and the weapons used. Regardless of the type of sparring your style engages in, you may find this to be the most challenging aspect of martial arts practice.

As we age, our body becomes less responsive. This change is most obvious during sparring, particularly if you spar with younger students. If you are an experienced martial artist, you will notice that you are a half beat slower than you used to be; that attacks that used to shock your opponents sometimes seem telegraphed; that counterattacks that used to score easily are sometimes too late to be effective. If you are new to sparring, you may be frustrated that younger students are faster or more flexible in sparring, even though you out-rank them. When your body begins to lose it's edge, it's time to put your mind to work for you. There are some simple principles that you can apply to just about any type of sparring to fight smarter.

MOBILITY

In sparring, mobility is used to test the waters and to avoid getting hit. When you initially face an opponent that you know nothing about, begin by moving around, left and right, forward and backward to test his response. Use short, quick motions and avoid fully committing your movements so you don't get countered. Notice if he tries to attack when you move in a certain direction. Notice whether he moves backwards or sideways when you move closer. Combine your movements with some light attacks or feints to gauge the strength of his response. Stay relaxed and ready to respond. Conserve energy at this stage, while keeping your opponent off guard and on the move.

Once the match is underway, mobility is essential to staying out of trouble. If you stand flat footed or plant your feet, you risk getting caught off guard by a strong attack. You also slow your attacks and counterattacks if you try to move from a dead stop. Because you have to first overcome inertia when starting from a standstill, your movements will not be explosive. Instead of standing around waiting for an opportunity, keep moving lightly on your feet, with a feeling of mentally and physically alert tension.

SIMPLICITY

Most good fighters have one or two simple techniques that are unbeatable—skills that they can fall back on no matter what. These skills are not fancy, complicated or showy. In fact, they may be "white belt" skills like a back fist, side kick, shoulder throw or arm bar. However, their execution is anything but white belt level. These techniques have been perfected to mastery level, allowing the fighter to use them at any time, in any situation, against any opponent. You can make this principle work for you when sparring against younger or more skilled opponents. Although you learn and practice a wide variety of skills, simple and complex, you should have two or three core skills to use when the chips are down.

ECONOMY OF MOTION

Wasted motion means wasted energy, something you cannot afford if you are sparring against younger classmates. By conserving energy, you have a better chance of tiring out your opponent and staying fresh long into a match. Movements that capitalize on economy of motion are small, direct and kinesthetically sound.

A good way to discover whether your movements are conserving or wasting energy is to video tape yourself sparring. When you watch the tape, notice whether you are expending energy for unnecessary movements like dropping your hands before you punch, shuffling your feet before you kick, or bouncing around without reason. Seeing yourself on video, and perhaps comparing yourself to an instructor or master of your style on tape, can help you weed out unnecessary movements that you might not even realize you are making.

RHYTHM

Every style of sparring has a rhythm to it and every fighter also has a preferred rhythm. Rhythm in sparring can be either consistent or broken. Most fighters are comfortable with a consistent rhythm, with techniques coming at similarly timed intervals. For example, a combination might be thrown in a 1-2-3 rhythm (jab, straight punch, kick) that gives equal emphasis to all three movements with equally timed intervals between movements. Skills delivered with a consistent rhythm are more likely to be anticipated and countered.

To lend an element of surprise to techniques, many fighters develop broken rhythm skills. Broken rhythm varies the strength or timing of movements and pauses, resulting in a 1—2-3 or 1-**2**-3 or 12—3 type attack. As a practical example, imagine the jab-punch-kick sequence above as a quick jab-punch combination followed by an extended pause during which your opponent relaxes slightly. As soon as you feel your opponent begin to relax (i.e. drop his hands, move his feet, etc.), you shift back and throw a quick kick to his midsection. The combination becomes 1-2-pause-3. If you have previously been using a 1-2-3 rhythm, your opponent should relax when the number 3 movement does not come as expected, giving you a perfect opening.

Using broken rhythm is an excellent means of fighting an opponent who is very quick because it disrupts his timing and frustrates him, allowing you to win out over his speed.

ANGULAR MOVEMENT

A common problem among novice fighters is a tendency to move only straight forward or straight backward. Although straight line movements are not necessarily bad, they are very predictable. If you find that you are walking into attacks or are getting chased backwards and hit with numerous attacks in combination, you need to add more angular movement to your sparring.

If you have difficulty entering your opponent's range for an effective attack or you find yourself walking into attacks, practice moving sideways to create openings. Circle to the left or right, forcing your opponent to keep moving. Most people are stronger at moving one way than the other. If you can find your opponent's weak side, you will be less likely to get hit on the way in and more likely to find a hole in his defenses. In addition to circling, you can move forward and then at an angle to pass your opponent or step out an angle and then move forward to attack. Experiment with different stepping patterns until you find what works for your body type and sparring style.

If you find that you are frequently the target of multiple combinations or spend a lot of time "running away" from opponents, you need to implement more sideways evasion steps in your sparring. The next time you spar, challenge yourself to never take more than one step straight backwards. Instead, focus on moving to the side or angling backwards by stepping backwards and out at a forty-five degree angle to the left or right.

COUNTERATTACKING

If you find that you do not have the speed or flexibility for a strong attack, you may be more successful with a counterattacking style of fighting. Every attacking technique requires your opponent to move from his safe "guard" stance and thereby exposes at least one opening. When you take advantage of this opening, it is called counterattacking.

Counterattacking is most successful when your opponent's attack is fifty to seventy-five percent complete. At this time, you opponent is most vulnerable because he is fully committed to and focused on his attack. He has little chance to retreat or change his attack midstream. For example, if your opponent throws a jab and you side step and counter with a kick to his knee, your kick will be most effective when he is in the midst of jabbing because he cannot block, move or counter your kick while his is still executing his punch. Once he has fully extended his punch, he can move out of the way or follow-up with another attack.

The same concept applies to grappling arts. Once your opponent has completed the transition into a lock or hold, you will have a hard time countering it. You have to apply your counter while he is in motion, before he attains a superior position.

Perception

Accurate perception, sometimes described as "reading" your opponent, can give you a few extra seconds to prepare a counterattack or spot an opening for an attack. Reading your opponent means watching both his weapons (feet, hands, knees, elbows, shinai, knife) and his cues (breathing, eye direction, hip rotation) to surmise what his next move might be. Even the best fighters have habits that can be used as cues. Some of the most common cues include:

1. Looking at the intended target before attacking.

2. Looking at the intended target and then quickly looking away before attacking.

3. Turning the body to face fully forward before attacking with the rear arm or leg.

4. Turning the body sideways before attacking with the lead arm or leg and before a spinning attack.

5. Momentarily raising or lowering the stance before attacking.

6. Frowning, grunting or changing the facial expression before moving to attack.

7. Breathing in before moving to attack.

8. Habitually repeating a tic or body movement before a specific attack, like dropping the shoulder before lunging in for a grab.

By carefully watching your opponent's weapons, you can block and avoid his attacks, but by watching the rest of his body, you can take advantage of the vulnerable spot in his attack and counter it.

DISRUPTION

Every opponent you face has a favored stance, a stance in which he feels very safe and which you have difficulty penetrating. Fortunately, there are certain points in time during sparring when your opponent is forced to disrupt his favored stance. He might be circling, switching stance or stepping forward to try to get a response from you. These movements are not part of the attacking or counterattacking that take place in the match, but more the incidental movements that fighters use to maintain distance or feel out an opponent. During these movements, certain openings inevitably appear like cracks in his armor. And even better than the openings themselves, is the fact that your opponent is most likely somewhat relaxed during these movements because there is a lull in the action. This is a perfect time to attack.

After a minute or two of sparring, you should be able to identify at least one movement pattern in your opponent. Perhaps he switches stance, steps in quickly and then back, circles to the left and then changes to circling right. Whatever the pattern, wait for him to initiate it and then attack. For example, after his quick step forward, as he starts to move back, rush him with a powerful attack and use his slight backward momentum to help knock him backwards. Or when you see him begin to initiate his forward step, move in with a powerful attack whose force will be doubled by his walking into it. You can find opportunities to disrupt your opponent's action before, during and after his attack. Disruption is truly the art of sparring that makes you untouchable when you have mastered it.

PAIN MANAGEMENT

The amount of contact allowed in sparring varies from none at all to almost anything goes, depending on the agreed upon rules in a match or class. In class situations, most schools practice some form of light to medium contact sparring to give students a taste of what getting hit feels like. A minority of schools spar full contact or non-contact at all times. No matter what the level of contact allowed, preparing yourself to manage the pain of contact sparring gives you an advantage.

There are certain areas of the body that can tolerate fairly strong blows through conditioning and practice including the stomach, chest, arms and legs. Other areas, including the face, groin, throat, and joints, cannot be conditioned and are always very painful when struck forcefully. For this reason, most martial arts do not allow attacks to these areas or only allow attacks only with the use of protection gear such as a groin cup or gloves.

Getting hit hard for the first time in sparring can be shocking. You may suddenly feel like you want to quit sparring, you may totally forget your strategy or you may have the urge to "get revenge" on your partner by hurting him. This is quite normal and will pass as you gain more experience. With experience, you will find that you are able to roll with the punches by relaxing, exhaling at the time of impact and allowing your body to absorb sparring blows without a lot of pain. Managing the pain means you do not let your emotions

254   Martial Arts After 40

take control, giving you the upper hand psychologically in any match. Of course, this doesn't mean fighting through crippling injuries. Remember hard strikes to the joints, groin and head/face can be serious and are good cause to stop sparring until you can assess the injury.

RANGE

Knowing your range and your opponent's range can help you select appropriate techniques as well as maintain a safe distance during sparring. Your range is the distance at which you feel you can comfortably attack. This may mean it is within arm's reach, within leg's reach, within one step, at the end of your stick or on your back with your opponent on top of you. Your range does not necessarily have to be far from or close to your opponent. Wherever you feel most comfortable is your range.

Each of your opponents also has a preferred range. Once you engage in sparring, the battle for range begins, with each of you trying to maintain the range at which you have more advantages, while preventing the other from doing the same. Depending on your opponent, your range may vary. You might feel more comfortable keeping a larger opponent closer to you while you might want to keep a faster, smaller opponent farther away. Use range to your advantage by developing techniques that widen your range (like footwork, feinting and lunging) and allow you to feel comfortable if it is shortened (effective countering skills). Avoid falling into the habit of working only at one range or in one favored stance because your opponents can quickly detect and exploit this habit.

INITIATION

A quick initiation can make up for a slower execution of an attack. Initiation is the movement that sets your attack in motion. It can be a step, lunge, lean, slide or something else entirely. Explosive initiations are commonly used by running backs in football and guards in basketball to outmaneuver defenders. You often see a guard take an explosive step by a defender, leaving the defender unable to recover in time to stop the penetration. The guard would probably not beat the defender in the fifty yard dash, but he knows how to get off one quick step to start his attack and that's all it takes to leave the defender flat footed.

In sparring, explosive initiation can leave your opponent flat footed as well. By the time he sees your attack coming, it is too late to defend against it. Speed in initiation comes from two sources: positioning and relaxation. If you are slow overall, you can use your body position for an edge. Before an attack, creep gradually closer to your opponent, so that you have cut a half step off his comfortable range. This doesn't mean take a half step forward all at once. Instead, gradually shuffle forward, move in a circling pattern toward your opponent or use some quick angular steps to cut the distance without obviously moving forward. Once you have cut the distance, initiate a quick direct attack. Your opponent will be surprised by the change in distance and find it hard to react appropriately.

If you can rely a bit more on your natural speed, you can create an explosive initiation from your normal attacking distance. The key lies in relaxation just prior to the attack. Many students tense up when trying to create explosive movements. Tensing actually slows you down because your muscles work against themselves. Just before you move, exhale about one third of your breath and fully relax your body. Then, without putting any tension in the attacking implement (such as the hand or foot), tense the initiator muscles only. For example, for an explosive kick, relax the foot and knee, but tense the large muscles of the hip, thigh and lower abdomen. Firing these large muscles drives the smaller muscles through a chain reaction, resulting in a faster movement than you can create by initially tensing the foot or knee. Once you initiate the movement, let it flow naturally to it's conclusion. Through practice, you will be amazed at how much you can increase your attacking speed by improving your initiation skills.

COMBINATIONS

Attacking and scoring with a single movement can be difficult if you don't have great speed. To make up for a lack of speed, you can use combination attacks. The more attacks you throw at an opponent, the more likely you are to score. The science of combinations is to open with one or two techniques to "soften up" the opponent and create an open target. Once you find an opening, follow up with at least one scoring technique. If you find it difficult to "break the ice", your attacks are often jammed or your opponent easily evades your attacks, effective combinations can strengthen your attacking repertoire.

The best combinations to start with are fundamental ones, such as those you learn from your instructor. There is a science to building combinations. Techniques should not be randomly strung together. As a general rule, combinations should be built so each technique takes advantage of the previous one. This might mean a low strike which causes the opponent to drop his guard is followed by a high strike to take advantage of the opening he creates in dropping his hands away from his head. Advanced combinations should include fakes, feints and footwork to create a specific response from the opponent. Good combinations try to predict the opponent's moves several steps ahead, like a chess match.

BE COUNTERINTUITIVE

Refusing to respond as your opponent's wishes is a good means of blunting his attack. Most fighters expect that if they move forward with an attack, their opponent will move backwards or side step. But what will they do if their opponent instead moves in closer? This is a counterintuitive movement and ruins the fighter's strategy. For example, if your opponent throws a series of quick jabs, instead of moving back out of range, move slightly to the outside of his arm and close the distance to strike him or clinch. Once you are past the end of his fist, he cannot continue to jab effectively because his striking weapon (fist) is now behind it's target (your head).

Being counterintuitive takes not just brains to figure out what might work, but guts, because the human brain is strongly conditioned to react in certain patterns. Strategies like moving into an attack rather than running away from it are directly counter to natural human safety instincts. And that's what makes them effective.

SET-UPS

In the advanced stages of sparring, you can implement the use of set-up techniques. In order for a set-up to work, you must first be sure that your opponent will respond predictably to an attack. If you find, in the course of a match, that your opponent always responds to your jab by ducking slightly, you can use the jab to set-up an upper cut to the jaw. Throw the jab, wait for your opponent to bring his head down and meet his dropping jaw with your rising uppercut.

By predicting your opponent's movement, you make your uppercut more effective and more likely to strike it's target. Set-ups work better when sparring with more advanced practitioners, because an advanced martial artist is more likely to know and consistently use the correct response to an attack, whereas a beginner might duck one time, step back the next and stand flat footed a third time. A set-up is a method of using the conditioned responses of your opponent against him.

TIMING

When you attack is as important as what technique you use.

Timing is not speed. Timing can be slow or fast. It is a matter of the appropriateness of attacking. There are certain times that are better to attack than others including:

1. When your opponent is in mid-step.

2. When your opponent changes stance.

3. When your opponent reacts to a feint, fake, draw or set-up technique.

4. When your opponent shifts his weight.

5. When your opponent is absolutely still.

6. After your opponent launches an attack but before he completes it.

7. When your opponent pauses between attacks.

8. As your opponent enters your range.

9. When your opponent moves backward.

10. When your opponent begins to inhale.

Timing comes from learning to recognize these opportunities and developing techniques to capitalize on them. You can benefit from practicing timing in slow motion with a partner. Take turns playing "the opponent" so each partner can practice reacting spontaneously to simulated sparring situations

COMMON MISTAKES IN SPARRING:

1. TOO MUCH BACKWARD MOVEMENT.

Taking more than one or two steps backward gives your opponent an advantage. In fact, taking any steps backward without a specific plan should be avoided. If you are just moving backward because you have nothing else to do, you have lost control of the match.

2. LACK OF FOOTWORK.

Standing flat footed makes you an easy target and slows your initiation speed. Keep moving lightly on your feet.

3. RELYING ON JUST A FEW SKILLS.

Having a few strong skills is essential in sparring, but relying only on a few skills or just one side of your body is dangerous. If your opponent figures out how to take away those skills with counterattacks, you may be in trouble.

4. BEING TOO TIGHT.

All too often, at a tournament, you see a fighter who gets in the ring looking like he's ready to bulldoze his opponent. Quite frequently, he ends up knocked out, tired out or injured before the first round is over. The best fighters are cool and collected when they step into the ring.

5. FAVORING THE RIGHT OR LEFT SIDE.

Being able to fight from both a left and right handed stance is an asset. While one stance may be stronger than the other and you should master techniques from your favored stance to rely on under pressure, strive to be proficient in fighting from both sides.

6. LACK OF FOLLOW-UP.

Rarely does a single technique win a match, or even score a point. Use combinations, footwork and feints to keep your opponent off guard. Do leave any opportunity un-scored.

7. POOR DISTANCING.

Know your range and use it. Standing too close to or too far from an opponent can render your techniques useless. Watch the centerline of your opponent, how wide his stance is and how quickly he moves in and out. Accordingly, adjust your distance.

8. LACK OF A PLAN.

Sparring is not brawling. You should have a plan when you start each match and do your best to stick to it and adapt during the match. Randomly whacking your opponent is too risky. Have at least a main plan and a backup plan going into each match.

9. POOR PERCEPTION.

Many novice fighters work their plan without regard to their opponent's actions. Stay in touch with your opponent and anticipate his movements.

10. FAVORING SPEED OVER TIMING AND RHYTHM.

Speed is useless if your opponent isn't there. Feel the opponent's rhythm, disrupt it and create your own tempo. Be in tune with the flow between yourself and your opponent so you can gauge the right time for action and inaction.

THINKING POINTS

1. Sparring can be a challenge for the over-40 student because younger students are naturally more flexible and faster. This deficit can be compensated through the use of strategy.

2. To maximize your sparring skills, stick to simple techniques.

3. In the early part of a match, use mobility combined with testing techniques to gauge the intent and skill level of your opponent.

4. Avoid moving straight forward and backward when angular movement is more appropriate.

5. Use observation as well as perception to determine your opponent's next move.

6. Disruption and broken rhythm can be used to level the playing field against more skilled or faster opponents.

7. A slow execution can be compensated for by a fast initiation.

8. Combination attacks can make up for a lack of speed in attacking.

9. There is an important difference between speed and timing. Understanding the right time to attack is critical.

Forms

Forms are called by many names, depending on the art you are learning, including kata, hyung, poomse, patterns, sets, and forms. Whatever the name, most traditional martial arts have forms. If you practice a form of karate, kung fu, tang soo do, tai chi, kenpo or taekwondo, you probably learn empty hand and/or weapons forms as part of your training. If you practice a modern or eclectic (mixed or hybrid) art like jeet kune do or sport grappling, you probably do not practice forms, although your instructor may adopt forms from other arts to practice. The traditional arts consider forms to be the backbone of the art, a chronicle of essential techniques handed down for centuries. Other arts consider forms useless, preferring to focus solely on sparring, self-defense or fighting techniques.

Most schools today fall somewhere in between, practicing forms for competition, demonstrations, aesthetic beauty, internal energy development, as a creative outlet, to practice basic techniques, for testing requirements or just for fun. If your school teaches forms, or if you choose to learn them on your own as a supplement to your formal training, there are a number of principles you can apply to improve your performance.

ACCURACY

Each movement in a form should be learned correctly before you begin to practice seriously. Once your body creates a muscle memory for a movement, it is difficult to unlearn it. Take your time in learning new forms. Pay specific attention to when a movement begins and ends, the intensity of energy in each technique and the speed of each segment.

Resist the urge to skip ahead or rush to finish the form just so you can say you know it from start to finish. Instead, make each new movement precise, crisp and focused. You will practice each form for many years after you learn it, so learning it well is more important than learning it quickly.

PACING

When you first learn a form in class, it will probably be as part of a group, performing according to your instructor's count or to the group cadence. You might practice one movement at a time, stopping to check your placement or to listen to instruction before moving to the next step. Once you have learned the steps to the form, you should think about their pacing. Not every movement is meant to be practiced with the same monotonous timing that you use when first learning it. Some movements are hard, some are flowing, some are quick, some are powerfully slow. The development of accurate pacing is part of the internalization of the form.

PUNCTUATION

Most forms have at least one shout (kiai or kihap) and sometimes as many as four or five. There may also be movements that are meant to be emphasized with powerful presentations or embellishments such as stomping the floor or striking the hand with a kick. These movements are meant to punctuate the form, much like a period or comma signals a pause in a paragraph. Give each punctuation point its proper attention to add to the drama and pacing of the form.

BREATH CONTROL

Movements in traditional forms are performed with either a quick forceful exhalation or a long controlled exhalation. Some styles breathe audibly, while others conceal breath sounds. Regardless of the breathing method you use, each breath should be planned and purposeful. By controlling your breathing, you can increase the power of your movements and improve your stamina during long or demanding form performances.

You can improve the ability to control the amount and intensity of exhaling by practicing one long exhalation or several short exhalations. Inhaling, however, should always be one smooth intake of oxygen.

POSTURE

The posture of traditional martial arts movements is different from that of sparring. In form practice there is more emphasis on the shape of each movement. Some movements are meant to be small and tight, others long and sweeping. Pay special attention to the alignment of your body, including your hips, knees, shoulders, neck and elbows, since each of these joints affects the placement of the rest of your body. If your hips are turned sideways instead of squared in front stance, your chest and arms will be twisted out of position. If your neck is not straight, your head will tilt to the side or look at the ground instead of focusing on your target. In forms practice, keep you upper body perpendicular to the ground unless your instructor specifically instructs you otherwise.

STANCE

The stances used in forms are very different from the stances used in fighting or self-defense. Form stances are the traditional stances of a style, often low and sometimes very impractical for fighting. Stances are the foundation of the form and accordingly they should be solid. When you move into a stance, you should end your step precisely in the stance, without shuffling your feet for position after you land. However, avoid getting so low into a stance that you cannot move comfortably to the next movement. Use your stances to project strength and stability without impairing your mobility.

INDIVIDUALITY

Each form you learn has elements that cannot be changed, including the structure and sequence of the movements. Yet, each student does a form slightly differently because of variations in body size, agility, flexibility, strength, and skill. Your performance naturally takes on it's own measure of individuality within the preset structure of the form. This individuality is what sets apart competitors who perform the same form in competition. If ten people do the same form, one or two always shine above the others because their individual interpretation of the form is superior. Try to use your individual strengths to enhance each form while maintaining its original structure and purpose.

MEMORIZING A NEW FORM

Learning a new form comes easy to some people and seems like organized torture to others. If you fall into the latter category, there are some tricks that can make learning new forms less stressful. If memorization of the movement sequence is a problem, try breaking the form down into small segments of no more than five movements. Learn and practice the first five movements.

Practice the sequence five times in the morning and five times at some point during the day. Just before bedtime, take five minutes to sit quietly and visualize the sequence in your mind. In three to five days, you will find that the first sequence of the form seems simple. This is the time to learn and add the second segment of up to five movements to your daily practice.

Continue practicing daily and adding segments until you complete the form.

An important consideration in breaking each form into segments is to make the segments logical groups of movements, not just break them down into sets of five. The first segment might work best as four movements, while the next might make sense grouped as five and the next as only two new (but complex) movements.

A very helpful training aid is a poster or hand drawn sketch that illustrates the movements of the form. You can hang up the poster in your practice area as a quick visual reference. You might even want to divide the segments as you learn them with a brightly colored magic marker to visually define your progress through the form.

During the initial stages of learning a new form, you should always face in the same direction, usually toward the front of the training area, so you can depend on visual cues like "turn toward the doorway" to aid your memorization. Once you have the sequence of movements memorized, practice the form facing in different directions, including starting out facing a corner of the room instead of facing a wall. By removing your visual cues, you develop a more internal sense of the sequence of turns and steps.

If you find this type of practice too confusing, go back and practice just segment one and then add segments as you master the form without visual cues, just as you did when you first learned it.

APPLICATIONS

Another way of practicing a form is to interpret the techniques so that you can create a situation in which the technique is applicable against an imaginary attack. By understanding how a sequence of movements can be applied to an opponent, you will be better able to perform and remember it. Applications can be learned from your instructor, from a video tape or from your own practice and imagination.

CREATIVE FORMS

Many modern martial arts styles, particularly those that encourage competition, allow advanced students to make up their own forms. Creative forms may be performed empty-handed or with a weapon. They are often performed to music for demonstrations or competition.

Creating your own form allows you to select movements that show off your strengths and eliminate those that you find uncomfortable. Even if your style does not encourage creative forms, making a form at home can add variety and fun to your practice.

BEYOND BOREDOM

Forms require hundreds or thousands of repetitions to master. Yet even the most disciplined martial artist finds endless repetition to be boring at times. Adding variety to your practice is a good way to beat boredom and stay on the road to mastery. Some ideas for varying your forms practice include:

1. Practice stances and steps only with no strikes or kicks. Pay special attention to your foot placement and the shape of your stances.

2. Practice each movement slowly using dynamic tension and slow exhalations.

3. Practice each movement with full power. Try to make your uniform "snap" with each technique.

4. Practice outdoors in the park or your yard.

5. Practice with a partner—take turns critiquing each other's performance.

6. Change the movements in the form. Replace every punch with a backfist or every kick with a punch.

7. Practice to music.

8. Add a weapon, such as the short or long stick. Replace the movements in the form with a corresponding weapons movement.

9. Try to get through the whole form without a mental break or mistake. Imagine your form as one movement and perform the entire form with the same mental state as you would perform a single punch.

10. Practice with your eyes closed. Try to follow the correct pattern of movement and end up in the same place that you started from.

THINKING POINTS

1. Forms are generally practiced in more traditional martial arts. Some martial arts that do not have traditional forms may practice creative or "borrowed" forms.

2. When learning a new form, concentrate on developing good habits over learning quickly.

3. The development of pacing and rhythm in a form is an important part of mastery.

4. Stances and posture for forms are very different than for sparring. Understanding the purpose of each movement can help you create an accurate performance.

5. Break new forms down into segments if you have difficulty memorizing them.

6. Practice a form in different directions to reduce your reliance on environmental cues and internalize the sequence of the movements.

7. Vary your practice to alleviate boredom brought on the by repetitious nature of form practice.

Weapons Training:
The Art of Short Stick

There are hundreds of martial arts weapons available for study ranging from the knife and stick to the sword and three section staff. Learning weapon techniques is an excellent means of expanding your martial arts study as you grow older. Weapons practice is less physically demanding than jumping kicks or breathtaking throws, but it is very challenging mentally. The road to learning the integration of your body and a weapon is filled with self-discovery.

While it is far beyond the scope of this book to cover a wide range of weapons, I would like to share the principles and techniques of one weapon that is easy to learn: the short stick. Its principles can be applied to many other weapons and its techniques can be applied to common everyday objects for self-defense.

A short stick, or joong bong, is a 30 to 36 inch long stick made of bamboo or rattan. It is a weapon that is easy to understand and simple to use. The fundamental nature of the joong bong is not that different from any other martial arts weapon. The simplicity and practicality of joong bong techniques make it easy to apply to common objects, such as a baseball bat, umbrella or cane, in a self-defense situation. It also provides the practitioner with fitness benefits: an enhanced sense of balance, speed and power control, agility and coordination.

Weapons practice is truly an art form. It helps you develop an aesthetic sense in a way that is different from kicking, striking or grappling practice. It opens up a new area of discovery and a new challenge to make yourself one with the weapon.

BENEFITS OF PRACTICE

The short stick is one of the most versatile weapons for self protection. It can be used against an unarmed and armed assailant. It is also a good companion for exercise to develop coordination, flexibility, speed, agility, precision, mental focus, and balance.

You can better understand your body and its relationships with your surroundings through joong bong practice: the effect of the gravity and its benefits, the principle of compensation in the movement of the human body, and the importance of centering and composure. Your sense of direction while in motion can be significantly enhanced through practicing a variety of blocks, thrusts, cuts, and strikes in sequence.

Due to the fact the force of the joong bong must be focused at the moment of impact, you will improve the ability to relax and concentrate at the moment when you need the power. For those who look for something different, short stick principles are universal. They can be easily adapted to any stylist or ability level of martial arts practice.

WEAPONS CONCEPTS

Every technique follows these seven steps:

1) assessment
2) relaxation
3) preparation
4) execution
5) impact
6) follow-through
7) repose

At stage one, you should assess the situation: the external circumstances and your internal condition relative to the technique you are about to perform. The external circumstances include how much space you have to execute a technique, your grip on the joong bong, your stance, your ability to move in each direction and whether you are practicing with a partner, practicing alone, or using a technique for self-defense. Your internal condition includes your mental focus, your preparedness to move quickly if necessary, your knowledge of the technique and your ability to adapt a technique to changing situations.

Relaxation, the second stage, denotes an alert preparedness to perform a technique. Your grip should not be overly tense, your shoulders should be relaxed and your stance should be light but firm. In this stage, you may need to retreat one step before proceeding with a technique to create more time and space to execute it.

The third stage is preparation, in which you should decide to attack first or wait and counterattack, assess what type of techniques are most suitable, control your breathing, and concentrate your muscular energy for the strike. All of this preparation happens in a split second.

The forth stage is execution: the primary response and the secondary response. The primary response includes evading, blocking, parrying, and cutting-in. The secondary responses are thrusting, striking, cutting, hooking, pushing, pulling, and locking.

The fifth stage is impact. Impact is more than hitting whatever target is available. It requires precision of the intended technique. The visual targets are the ones that you see with your eyes, but the actual targets are one to two inches beneath the surface. When you hit the target precisely your technique generates less noise but severe pain to the opponent.

The sixth stage is the follow-through in which you feel the vibration of your attack and the response of the opponent's body. It is also called the "death echo" which comes after you strike the opponent successfully. It can be compared to the heightened but soft sensation after you have just hit a home run in baseball. Your weapon should not be like a hammer that nails, but rather like an extension of your finger as it presses a vital point.

The seventh stage is the repose. You must always practice reposing (returning to a ready position) after you attack. Repose whenever you have finished your intended attack so that your mind stays alert and your body is ready to execute another technique immediately, if necessary.

FUNDAMENTAL TECHNIQUES

GRIP

A joong bong has four parts: bottom (mit), tip (kut), grip (jabi), and body (tah). First position your little finger approximately 2 inches above the bottom of the joong bong (in the grip area) with your ring and middle finger wrapped firmly around the stick and your index and thumb encircling it gently. Aim the tip at the throat of your opponent and keep the bottom pointing at the middle of your front leg (thigh). Your gripping elbow should be slightly bent with the angle of your arm and the joong bong at approximately 120 degrees. Position the joong bong at the center of your stance in front of you.

STANCE

There are five fundamental stances in joong bong practice: attention, neutral, front, back, and counter-cut stance.

Attention stance: Grip the joong bong upside down in your left hand (if you are right handed) with tip facing down and the bottom up. Put your joong bong at the left side of your waist at a 60 degree angle. Put both feet together with your right hand naturally resting on the right side.

Front stance: When you attack or defend at a very close range, you need to shift your weight onto your lead leg to magnify the power of the strike or the block. Straighten your upper body perpendicular to the ground and stretch your rear leg so that it can support your force.

Neutral stance: From the attention stance, move your left foot backward one step, grasp the grip with your right hand and pull it out in front of you. If you are holding the joong bong in your right hand, position your right foot in front and left foot in the back. Your front foot can be placed at approximately an angle of 15 degrees. The angle between your front foot and back foot is about 60 degrees (The angles may vary depending on your personal preference.). Your left hand should be placed directly in front of your left thigh, about one foot away from your waist in a relaxed guard. Your weight should be equally distributed on both legs to prepare for movement in any direction.

Back stance: When you back up, your body weight moves to your rear leg. Back stance is used only briefly avoid losing the advantage in a confrontation. Use it as a quick transition for strategic movements. As soon as you accomplish the transition from a defensive position, change your stance immediately from back stance to front stance, or at least to neutral stance.

Counter-cut stance: This is very close to the shape of cat stance. The difference is that your weight should be equally distributed on both legs and you should squat slightly with your upper body forward. This stance is mostly used when you have no time to retreat and must counter strike in place.

GUARD

There are three types of guard positions: middle, low, and high guard.

Middle guard position: Position the joong bong in front of you with the tip aiming at the neck of the opponent. Middle guard position is used in most cases to prepare for combat (as in the neutral stance).

Low guard position: Place the joong bong behind your rear leg in back stance to conceal the weapon behind your body.

High guard position: Bring the joong bong behind your body above your head with the other hand aiming to the front. This technique is used to exaggerate your height and size for a counterattack.

Footwork

There are seven types of footwork: forward, backward, inside, outside, left turn, right turn, and full turn step.

Forward step: Move your front foot forward and the rear foot follows.

Backward step: Move the rear foot backward and let the front follow.

Inside step: Move your rear foot to the inside direction and let the other foot follow.

Outside step: Move your front foot to the outside direction and let the other foot follow.

Left turn step: Move your rear foot ninety degrees counterclockwise and turn your body accordingly, pivoting on your front foot.

Right turn step: Move your rear foot ninety degrees clockwise and turn your body accordingly, pivoting on your front foot.

Full turn step: Move your rear foot one step forward, then with the momentum pivot the other foot and turn your body 180 degrees.

DEFENSIVE SKILLS

There are five fundamental defensive skills: high, low, inside, outside, and cross block.

High block: From the middle guard position, raise the joong bong to a few inches above your head, with the other hand positioned in front of you as a guard or to grab the opponent.

Low block: From the middle guard position, drop the tip of the joong bong in circular motion parallel to the outside line of the front thigh. Position your other hand in front of you in a guard position.

Inside block: Move the joong bong inward, to cover your body against your opponent's attack. The angle can vary according to the circumstances. Move the other hand along with the blocking hand.

Outside block: Move the joong bong outward, approximately six inches to a foot, to cover your body against your opponent's attack. The angle can vary. Move the other hand along with the blocking hand.

Cross block: From the middle guard position, raise the joong bong a few inches above your head with your forearm across your face. Position your other hand in front of you as a guard.

Offensive skills

There are seven joong bong offensive skills: straight strike, thrust, inside cut, outside cut, hook, reverse thrust, and locking.

Straight strike: From the middle guard position, bring the joong bong straight above your head at the center. Bring the tip of the joong bong all the way down to your spine. At this time bring your other hand in front of you to cover your vital points. Then bring back your other hand and the joong bong to the original position slicing the air, with the striking area of the joong bong landing on top of the skull of the opponent.

Thrust: From the middle guard position, push the tip of the joong bong into the opponent's eyes or the center of his neck. Use your other hand to support the thrusting hand.

Inside cut: From the middle guard position, loop the joong bong clockwise and swing it diagonally, with both hands, to the inward direction.

Outside cut: From the middle guard position, loop the joong bong counterclockwise and swing it diagonally, with both hands, to the outward direction.

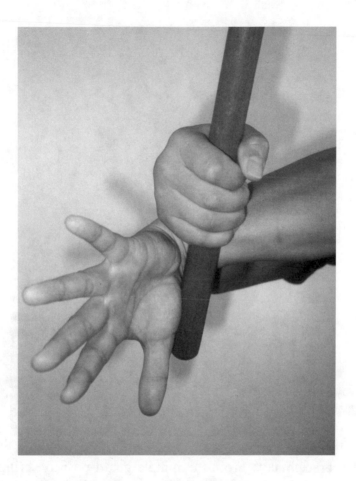

Hook: The hook is used to control the opponent's limb. For example, grab the wrist of your training partner, insert the bottom of the joong bong behind his triceps and hook the arm down toward you.

Reverse thrust: From the middle guard position bring the tip of the joong bong toward you and grab the body of the joong bong with your other hand and thrust the bottom of the weapon into the solar plexus.

Locking: Locking is used to disarm, immobilize or disable an opponent. There are hundreds of locking techniques and variations that can be performed with the joong bong. For example, from the middle guard position, grab the wrist of your training partner with your left hand and twist slightly outward. Insert the tip of the joong bong under his or her armpit. Place the body of the weapon on his neck and press the vital points in the neck.

VITAL TARGETS

The primary targets for joong bong attacks are the head and neck. The secondary targets are the arm, trunk, and lower limbs.

For striking techniques, the targets are the top of the skull, temples, jaw, neck, wrists, forearms, elbow, rib cage, knee, shin, calf, and ankle. The vital striking areas for thrusting techniques are the eyes, temples, neck, solar plexus, rib cage, lower abdomen, thigh, calf, and instep.

ADVANCED SKILLS

The skills described so far are the building blocks for all joong bong techniques and applications. Once you have learned the basic offensive and dcfensive skills, there are hundreds of combat applications, patterns, and combinations that can be practiced alone or with a partner. Joong bong skills can be practiced for self-defense, personal improvement or artistic value. This section has covered a small sample of the most basic skills to give you an idea of what is possible with the joong bong. If you would like to pursue joong bong practice further, there are several video tapes available from Turtle Press (www.turtlepress.com) that detail the basic movements, patterns, combat applications and the more advanced art of the double stick (using two sticks at once).

THINKING POINTS

1. Weapons training is well suited for older practitioners because it is less physically demanding, but more mentally challenging than other areas of practice.

2. The integration of the weapon with your body is a process of self-discovery.

3. Weapons practice increases balance, speed, power control, coordination and overall fitness.

4. Each weapon skill can be broken down into seven conceptual stages.

5. Weapons skills, like empty-handed skills, include stance, footwork, blocks, strikes, and locks. Weapon skills also require the understanding of grip, guard and the positioning of the empty hand in relation to the weapon.

chapter 22

5 Elements of Success in Martial Arts

#1. COMPENSATE INEQUALITY

Accept that all people are not born genetically equal for martial arts, but you can compensate for your weaknesses. For example, long legs and arms are the genetic predisposition for skilled kickers and punchers. In sparring, however, it is not a contest of whose kicks reach further, but it is a game of positioning, hitting, and timing. Even if you do not have such natural advantages as speed and timing, you can develop a good sense of hand and eye coordination or flexibility which can compensate for missing elements. Conversely speaking, if you are not a tall, flexible person, you can develop speed. If you are not as fast as you would like to be, you can counterbalance it by improving your ability to anticipate the opponent's movement.

#2. ACQUIRE THE DESIRED PHYSICS OF TECHNIQUES

One of the best ways to understand the engineering aspect of techniques is to observe the performance of your master or top practitioners in your style. From the beginning to the end, visualize the procedure or draw the movement on a piece of paper. If you look at the technique this way, there is not much room for error. It will also help you internalize the technique so that you can provide your own feedback while you practice. By understanding the physics of a skill and having the proper engineering in your techniques, you can correct technical problems.

#3. BLOCK UNDESIRABLE FACTORS OUT OF YOUR MIND

Under ideal conditions, your muscles can function naturally, without any hindrance. In reality, there are always vast numbers of distractions that affect the way you feel and, therefore, the way you perform. Those factors impact your brain, which in turn affects your muscles' responses, resulting in poor performance. Concentrate on the immediate goal of the moment in order to block undesirable factors out of your mind. The way you process your performance internally will determine the way you act physically. Try to stay firm and demonstrate to yourself that you have the inner qualities to do well under pressure.

#4. DO IT WITH THE RIGHT ATTITUDE

Martial arts practice does not simply mean beating your opponent. It involves more than physical engagement. What matters is the way you process what you do internally and how you express your internal processes. Your psychological attitude is critical in martial arts performance. Losing your temper or controlling your emotions comes from your attitude— the ability to view yourself with perspective. It is a sign of self-confidence. With the right attitude, you can be highly attuned to your performance.

#5. ISOLATE "WHAT IS" FROM THE EMOTION OF THE SITUATION

Practice exposing yourself to potential surprises and the anxiety of the unknown while maintaining equilibrium and focusing on the factors that are important. By facing stressful situations you can learn that there is nothing special to fear no matter how high the pressure might be. After a while you can be fairly sure that you can perform comfortably under pressure. When you can isolate what "is" from your emotional reaction to a situation, you are capable of subduing your opponent. Your muscles will be recruited in the same effective way that you perform in a stress-free situation. You may even grow to enjoy the pressure. Try to perform accurately in every practice, win or lose, under stressful and stress-free circumstances.

1. Look for ways to compensate for your personal weaknesses or shortcomings.

2. Through observation and visualization, you can produce an error-free performance.

3. Take an engineer's viewpoint of each technique to remove technical flaws.

4. During practice, focus on what you are doing rather than external stimulus.

5. Try not to color situations with emotional bias.

chapter 23

Your **Mind-Body Connection**

For centuries, martial arts has been known as a means of unifying the mind and body. However, unless you are specifically including exercises in your training that promote the development of the mind-body connection, you may not be reaping the full benefits that the arts have to offer. As an older martial artist, your goals most likely lie more in the areas of self-improvement or spiritual development rather than becoming a tournament champion or doing flying, spinning kicks. To reach these goals, there are several types of activities you can make a part of your training schedule, including meditation and relaxation exercises.

MEDITATION

Meditation is often practiced before or after martial arts class. Although most martial arts instructors know that meditation is helpful for students, few know the concrete benefits that meditation can bring. Regular meditation's primary benefit is to counteract stress by:

❑ relaxing the blood vessels and lowering blood pressure

❑ slowing the heart rate

❑ slowing the breathing rate

❑ decreasing sweating

❑ reducing the pulse rate (even while not meditating)

❑ reducing anxiety

Of course, you can only reap these benefits if meditation is done consistently and correctly. If you have never learned to meditate, follow these steps to get started:

1. Set aside 10 to 20 minutes a day during which you can have completely undisturbed time. You may want to do this right before or after martial arts class, when you wake in the morning or just before bedtime.

2. Find a comfortable place to sit, either in a straight backed chair or on the floor with your legs crossed. Lightly rest your hands on your knees. Relax and get comfortable.

3. Close your eyes. Some people find it helpful to meditate on a specific word or sound while others like to just let their mind be empty and free. Use which ever method works best for you.

4. As stray thoughts enter your mind, just let them pass by. Do not judge them or try to banish them. Just let them be.

5. As you become more comfortable with meditating, you will increasingly find your mind adjusting to meditation and will be less distracted by stray thoughts. Enjoy the peace and calmness that meditation brings.

All sorts of thoughts will come into your mind and go away. Some stay and some attract your attention. Don't try to grab any thought with your conscious mind. Let them come, be and go. Be mindful but don't be attached to any of them including yourself—the sitting being. Gradually pain and conscious thoughts will disappear. You will enter the deep sea of awakened unconsciousness. You will experience peace with yourself and surroundings.

6. Breathe slowly in through your nose, expanding your belly with each breath. Briefly hold your breath and then let it out through your mouth, gently contracting your belly and fully emptying your lungs. As your meditation progresses, your breathing rate will slow to as low as six breaths per minute. Some people like to count as they breath—counting up to inhale and down to exhale.

7. Relax and enjoy each meditation session. There is really no wrong or right way to do it as long as you are relaxed and feel refreshed after each session.

Meditation is a very personal experience. It's benefits can be significant and long lasting. When you meditate, your blood pressure goes down and your heart rate drops. It is reported that meditation is twice as effective in lowering oxygen consumption compared to sleep. It slows your breathing from the normal of fourteen breaths per minute to six breaths or less per minute. Anxiety, depression and agitation are often significantly diminished after 2 to 4 weeks of daily meditation.

RELAXATION IN YOUR MOVEMENTS

Tension is positive and necessary for human movement. It generates power. However, when you hold tension internally, your muscles get tight and constrain your movements. It also leaves you susceptible to injury. Physical tenseness can be an outward manifestation of stress or inner tension. If you find that your movements are very tense, you may need to work on total body flexibility and relaxation before proceeding with other areas of training. Practicing a series of daily relaxation exercises can help relieve both mental and physical tension.

The first step in releasing tension in your movements is to select a few simple movements, such as a segment of a form. Practice them repeatedly in the same sequence. As you practice, try to discover the possible causes of tenseness or hindrance in your movements. Ask yourself the following questions:

❖ Is your back too tight?
❖ Are you putting too much power in your extremities?
❖ Are your shoulders tense and hunched?
❖ Is your stance short or constricted?
❖ Do your movements stop short of their full range of motion?
❖ Are your heels raised off the floor in deep stances?
❖ Are your knees stiff and unyielding?
❖ Is your breathing too short or too hard?
❖ Are your fists clenched too tightly?

As you practice repeatedly and mindfully, you will be able to identify the sources of these problems and adjust yourself to eliminate restrictions in your movement. The following practice process is helpful in discovering problem areas.

1. SLOW DOWN

Move slowly so that you experience the natural elasticity and responsiveness of your muscles and joints. Slow practice increases sensation, range of movement, and a reasonably strenuous but pleasurable sensation in the muscles and joints.

2. BREAK DOWN EACH MOVEMENT INTO SMALL SEGMENTS

In your first attempt at a sequence, try to move each body part separately and slowly with the least amount of effort. Feel the different sensations of every single inch of the movement. This process brings you at least two results: it helps your body find its own dynamic center and it helps you feel restrictions and hindrances more clearly. Take your time and explore your body through new ways of movement.

3. RESYNTHESIZE THE MOVEMENT INTO A SINGLE UNIT

As you advance, focus on being conscious of the movement of your whole body as one unit and incorporating breathing exercises while you move.

4. CHANGE THE SPEED

Experiment with your body's ability to move at varying speeds. Move as fast as you can, move fast at the beginning and slow at the end, start slowly and pick up speed gradually, moderate your speed throughout the movement—experiment freely with speed so you can understand the relationship between the technique and your body. Try to find the ideal balance between speed and tension.

5. CHANGE THE TENSION

Change the tension levels of the movement consciously. Try doing the technique with slow, controlled tension and with relaxed speed. Purposely tighten your muscles and then purposely relax them so you can internalize the different feelings evoked by tense movements.

6. INTEGRATE YOUR KNOWLEDGE AND DISCOVERIES

The final stage of discovery is to combine all the knowledge and understanding you have gained from these exercises while you are performing in class, rather than in controlled practice conditions.

ACCUPRESSURE

Accupressure is a pressure applied to acu-points on the surface of the body. Acu-points are small energy centers that are sensitive to pressure. In martial arts training these points are used as vital points to subdue the opponent. By applying hard pressure abruptly to a point, you can inflict severe pain or even unconsciousness. These same points can be stimulated through a more gentle application of pressure to un-block and regulate the energy flow at certain points in the body in which energy often stagnates, becomes depleted or accumulates in excess.

In the practice of healing accupressure, organs are believed to be energy subsystems within the entire energy system. Activation of a particular point causes reflex responses in another part of the body that corresponds to that point. Accupressure is believed to prevent illness and reduce pain because it triggers the release of the body's own healing drugs such as endorphins and enkephalins.

MERIDIANS

A meridian is specific but invisible channel through which energy flows. They are complex energy networks distributed throughout the body connecting terminals to other terminals. As one channel ends, another one begins. If you compare the body to the electrical system, the meridian is like the wiring whereas the acu-points are like the light bulbs. There are over fifty meridians in the body. It is believed that by stimulating the meridians, you can prevent illness or diminish pain.

THE ENERGY CENTER

The most powerful energy and communication center of the body is believed to be the abdominal cavity in which the liver, kidneys, bladder, spleen, and other vital organs are housed. It is the beginning point of the umbilicus through which we first begin to breathe, receive nutrition, and excrete wastes as a fetus. If any problem occurs in this region, it can affect everything else in the body. It acts as the seat of control for continuation of life from fetus to old age. The lymphatic, circulatory, and nervous systems all cross paths in this area. The meridians and organs of digestion, assimilation, and elimination also go through this region. It is the energy generator.

Both accupressure and martial arts acknowledge the importance of this area. Many traditional Eastern martial arts practice breathing methods to enhance the strength of this energy center where *ki* or *chi* is believed to originate.

MORNING ACCUPRESSURE

If you find that your body is tense or stiff in the morning, try a quick course of do-it-yourself accupressure to invigorate your systems.

1. Remember that the major meridians all cross paths in the region of your stomach, so begin with gentle pressure to your naval area for ten repetitions, with deep slow breathing each time.

2. Then squeeze your arm firmly from the wrist to the shoulder. Do the other side the same way.

3. Sit and press your leg muscles along the center line with your thumb. You may do both legs at the same time.

4. Circulate your ankle in and out ten times.

5. Press the bottom of your foot firmly with both of your thumbs to intensify the force. Press around the entire bottom. Repeat the same procedure with the other foot.

6. Turn your head from side to side to release tension in your neck.

7. Firmly slap your shoulders with your palm to relieve tension.

8. Squeeze your hand firmly a few times, alternating sides.

9. Finally, inhale deeply for a count of 10 - 15 and exhale for a count of 10-15. Do it five to ten times.

10. Now get up and get started on the day!

THINKING POINTS

1. The enhanced mind-body connection often attributed to martial arts must be consciously worked toward.

2. Meditation has many benefits, both within and beyond martial arts practice. Setting aside even 15 minutes a day can have a positive effect.

3. Tension is an obstacle that can prevent the formation of a deep mind-body connection, however it can be reduced through the use of exercises and relaxation techniques.

4. Relaxation must be a daily conscious choice. A few hours of martial arts practice each week will not bring satisfactory results.

5. Accupressure can help you get in touch with and invigorate your body.

6. Acu-points can create both positive and negative effects on the body depending on how they are stimulated.

chapter 24

When the Going Gets Tough

As an older martial artist, there will be times in your training when you face special challenges related to your age and the circumstances it brings. View these challenges, not as obstacles or end-points, but as learning opportunities, as ways to expand your horizons in the martial arts.

HOW TO BALANCE FAMILY, TRAINING AND WORK

As you approach and move through middle age, your family may be putting increasing demands on your life. Instead of coming home from work, grabbing a quick dinner and heading off to martial arts class for the night, you may find yourself being pulled in all directions. If you are part of a two career family, you may find that you have to take the children to practices and club meetings or baby-sit when your spouse is out. Your martial arts class schedule will often be in direct conflict with your son's t ball games or your daughters violin recital. And if you are working late one or two nights a week on top of it all, getting martial arts classes may begin to seem impossible.

There are several solutions to balancing your martial arts training with the rest of your life:

1. Communicate. If martial arts is very important to you, explain this to your family and discuss exactly what training schedule is the most convenient for everyone. You may have to make some sacrifices like taking on extra baby-sitting time on the weekend or giving up a night out with your friends in exchange for your family's agreement to give you two or three undisturbed class periods during the week. If your family has difficulty understanding the amount of time you devote to martial arts, explain the benefits to the family, such as your reduced stress level, your increased fitness, or your improved discipline at work.

2. Ask your family or your children to join you. Martial arts classes can be enjoyed by people of all ages and are healthy family-oriented activities. The more family members who are attending class with you, the easier it will be to get to class on a regular schedule. An alternative is to join a class that offers child-care services during class time (such as at a health club) so you can take young children with you.

3. Join an early morning or late night class. By scheduling your training time during your family's "off-peak" time, you will not be taking away from family time for martial arts. Many schools have early morning, late night or lunch time classes.

4. Practice at home. Skip one class a week and practice at home instead. You can involve your children in your practice by letting them hit a target and practice some simple skills or you can take them to the park and practice while you watch them play.

5. Prioritize. Perhaps you are having trouble finding time for class because you have too many other activities on your plate. If you are playing in a recreational softball league, volunteering for the school board, training for a 10K race and coaching your son's little league team in addition to martial arts, you should drop one or two activities for a while.

6. Cut back. If you are a black belt, you may be taking on teaching duties in addition to training a few times a week. With family responsibilities, this can become difficult to manage. Talk with your instructor about cutting back your teaching schedule during busy times, like your daughter's soccer season or when you have a big project at work.

Many students grow frustrated and give up their martial arts classes rather than trying to work out a suitable schedule with their family. This is a shame because martial arts can truly benefit you, and in turn, your whole family. If you find yourself struggling to get to class, talk honestly with your family and your instructor to actively seek a solution.

GETTING FAMILY SUPPORT

1. Let your family know that your training is important to you and you are committed to it. Ask for their support.

2. Support family members in activities that they care about in the same that you would like them to support you.

3. Ask for support in specific ways to make it easier for your family to help you.

4. Set clear boundaries between work, training and family time.

5. Schedule time each week to organize and prioritize family life and activities for the week. Be willing to compromise and ask other family members to do the same.

6. Express your gratitude and appreciation for your family's support.

7. Share your accomplishments with your family. Invite them to promotion tests, competitions, demonstrations or award ceremonies.

8. Point out ways that your training makes you a better spouse, parent or family member.

9. Communicate with your family when you are having difficulty.

LIVING WITH CHRONIC INJURIES

By the time you reach forty or fifty years old you have probably suffered at least one serious injury in your lifetime. Perhaps it was the result of a car accident or a work related mishap, a slip on the ice or an old sports injury. Whatever the cause, past injuries can interfere with your martial arts training and even your daily life. As you age, previously healed joint or bone injuries may show up again as arthritis, bursitis, tendonitis or achy joints on rainy days. These conditions are often difficult to heal fully and can worsen with inactivity or overuse.

If you have a chronic injury, the first step to dealing with it is to accept that you cannot fix it or will it away. Some days you will have to stay home instead of going to class. Some days you will have to go easy when you would rather break a good sweat with the rest of your classmates. Chronic injuries should not be approached with a "no pain, no gain" attitude. The more you push, the worse they get whereas a day or two of rest can give you weeks of pain free training time. Listen to your body and know when to take it easy.

The second important step is to take an active approach to managing your injury. See an orthopedic doctor or physical therapist who can help you design a daily program of rehabilitative exercises. Many joint injuries recur because the muscles surrounding the joint are not strong enough to handle the demands you are placing on them. If the muscles cannot handle the work load, they transfer it to the joints, often resulting in chronic pain. This starts a downward spiral of pain leading to inactivity which weakens the muscles further leading to more pain.

The key to stopping this pattern is to strengthen the muscles through a course of isotonic and isometric exercises. Many of the exercises your physician or therapist prescribes may seem too easy or without much benefit. Do not skip them just because they seem easy. Follow the plan you receive exactly and listen carefully to the instructions on how to perform each exercise, even if you think you already know how to do it. Make your rehabilitation plan a daily habit, a daily gift to your aching joints or muscles. You will be amazed at the results a couple of weeks of well planned strengthening and stretching brings.

Once you start feeling better, do not drop your exercise program. Instead, visit your physical therapist again and talk about a long-term maintenance program to keep your muscles strong and ward off pain in the future.

DEALING WITH INSTRUCTOR AGE BIAS

Age bias can take many forms from blatant to sublime. At one extreme you may encounter an instructor who tells you that you are simply too old to take lessons. At the other end of the spectrum, your instructor may appear to be comfortable with your age, but subtly demonstrates his bias by never pairing you with the most talented students in class or lowering his expectations of you at promotion time.

Your first line of defense against age bias lies in your initial choice of a school and instructor. When you visit a school, observe the class and note the age range of the students. Are there many students your age or older? Are they doing the same activities as the rest of the class? Does the instructor seem to make exceptions to the curriculum for them or have them sit out portions of the class? While older students may not be able to excel at all martial arts activities, their instructor should encourage them to try their best and keep striving to improve.

After observing class, talk to the instructor. Ask if there are any age related requirements or exceptions to the curriculum. Try to get a feeling for his or her expectations of you as a student. A good instructor will expect you to work at your full potential while understanding shortcomings or individual needs that you may have. In this respect, you might be more comfortable with an instructor close in age to your own.

If you are already and active martial artist who is experiencing age bias in class, you may have a more difficult time resolving your frustration. Some instructors feel that are doing you a favor by going easy on you, pairing you with less skilled partners or not teaching you difficult skills. Their intentions are well meaning, however, the results can range from frustration to humiliation. If you feel that this is the case with your instructor, take a minute after class to talk with him about it.

Rather than accusing him of discrimination, choose a specific incident from class and point out how it might have been handled differently. For example, you might say "I enjoy sparring with Bill because we're close in age, but I would love to have a chance to spar with some of the other blue belts too. What do you think I need to improve before I'm ready for that?" This question gives your instructor a chance to save face by saying, "Yeah I think you're ready for that too, how about next class?" or "You need to work on your counterattacking a bit more, here's what to practice." By opening up a constructive dialogue, you give your instructor the opportunity to see that you are eager to push yourself harder. Once you point this out, he may feel more comfortable pushing you as well.

In a rare case, you may encounter the opposite of an overly cautious instructor. You may have the misfortune to meet up with an instructor who wants to prove that you really are too old for his class by pushing you beyond your limit. This is a potentially dangerous situation. If you find yourself in this unfortunate position, seek out another, more understanding instructor at your earliest opportunity. It is not worth getting injured to prove yourself to this kind of instructor.

GETTING ALONG WITH YOUNGER CLASSMATES

The majority of martial arts students today are under the age of 25 which means you may find that you are one of the oldest members of class. Since martial arts emphasizes personal development and respect for others, this should not be a problem. You will generally find that other students are respectful of you regardless of your age or ability level. Occasionally, though, you may run into a younger student who wants to test you or give you a hard time.

Problems with younger students are most likely to occur in sparring or self-defense. A certain student might kick too hard or is out to beat up on you rather than work with you in practice. When you find yourself in this situation, first point out the problem to your partner in a casual way. Try something like "Let's go a little easier on the throws." or "I'd like to take this drill a little slower so I can work on form rather then speed." If you partner was inadvertently being too rough, this should solve the problem. If it does, take a moment to thank your partner afterwards for working at a comfortable level.

What if you point out the problem to your partner and he continues doing it? Your best option is to speak with your instructor privately after class. Mention that you don't feel comfortable working with this particular student and would like to be paired with a different partner in future classes. In many cases, you may not be the only person who is having problems with a particular student. Some students are in class for the wrong reasons. By bringing the problem to your instructor's attention, you are helping him manage class better, not just idly complaining.

COMPETITION

Many martial arts styles encourage students to enter competitions as a way of testing their skill level or for personal enjoyment. Unlike many years ago where forty-year-olds competed in the same division with twenty-year-olds, most competitions now have senior, executive or golden senior divisions. This means you will be competing against people of a similar age. Depending on the size of the tournament, there may be a single senior division for students ages 35 and older or there may be several senior divisions broken into age groups like 35 to 44, 45 to 54 and over 55.

Before entering a competition, ask about the age brackets. Competing against students in a similar age bracket levels the playing field and allows you to enjoy competition at any age.

CHANGING SCHOOLS

Moving to a new school can be as difficult as moving to a new home or starting at a new job. Often, the students at your martial arts school become your second family. You come to learn what they expect from you and you also come to rely on them. A comfortable rapport is developed over time that can be difficult to let go when it is time to move on.

Even more difficult can be finding a new school that will let you pick up where you left off. Changing schools may mean starting over at white belt or having to test to keep your rank. It also means having to learn the etiquette, customs, and unwritten rules. This can be harder than it was when you took up classes as a beginner because over time you have established habits and expectations that will have to be adapted.

The first few weeks at a new school are always challenging, so keep an open mind and try to fit in. You may find that some students resist letting you into their inner circle or question your rank or the way you do certain techniques. Be polite but don't get intimidated. As long as you follow your new instructor's directions, you do not need to worry too much about what the other students think about your skill level. Stay positive and give your new school at least four to six weeks evaluation time before you decide whether or not it is a good fit.

THINKING POINTS

1. In mid-life a wide variety of commitments can make it difficult to keep up a regular schedule of martial arts classes. Find ways to compromise with your family and prioritize your schedule.

2. A part of successfully growing older as an athlete is accepting and actively dealing with past or chronic injuries. Taking an aggressive approach to staying well and knowing when to take a day or two off are critical to enjoying martial arts for many years to come.

3. Age bias from instructors and class mates is not something you have to tolerate grudgingly. When you experience age bias, take action by pointing out the problem and suggesting a positive solution.

4. Competitions are now open to students of all ages. Before you register for an event, ask about the availability of senior or executive divisions.

BOOK IV:
MASTERY POINTS

Mastery Points

This final section is a collection of Mastery Points for the advanced martial artist. As you grow older, in life and in the arts, you may find that many books you pick up are focused on the how-to's and the what-to's of martial arts, but lack something deeper that you are now searching for. It is natural, as we age, to become more introspective, to search for meaning and connections, where before we were happy to learn skills and techniques. Mastery Points are beyond technique, yet they are the essence of technique.

Each mastery point is a universal concept, theory or rule that applies across all martial arts, and in fact across all human movement. They are not meant to be taken in any special order or to be understood at face value. When you are ready, when you have reached the right point in your journey, you will understand them. Until that time, read one that seems to speak to you, one whose title makes sense to you or intrigues you (not more than one a day) and think about it. Some of the points may seem obvious and simple. Others may seem unfathomable or senseless. Contemplate each one without judgment or bias. Try to apply it to your practice, to understand and internalize it. Try to prove and then disprove it in your training. Turn it inside out and upside down. Look it in the eye and challenge it. Then let it go and wait. When you've got it, you'll know.

Mastery Point One

Surrender: Don't Control

Before you engage in physical activity, take a few moments to sit, stand or lie back with your eyes closed. Simply wait and listen for impulses, inner sensations, sounds, or energy that arises uncensored from deeper levels within you. Thoughts, feeling or images emerge from deep inside you. Let them lead you into movement. You should surrender yourself to movement instead of controlling it.

When you stop controlling your movements, you can discover how your body prefers to move. By surrendering your conscious self to the unconscious flow, you naturally shift out of old, unnatural and less effective patterns into new, fresh and creative movements. Spontaneous movement helps you deal with your physical limitations, pain or apathy toward training.

Each time, feel the special quality of the presence of your own liveliness rather than merely moving around. Be aware of what a particular movement quality awakens in you. Do not be judgmental. Keep your mind wide open to any possibility to explore qualities that you have not previously been exposed to. Stay true to your own inner impulses. Be as you are rather than as you think someone else wants you to be. Accept yourself as you are. Allow yourself to access the richness of your own inner world. Let your mind communicate with your body. Let your movement be conscious of what has been unconscious. Surrender yourself to what arises and face it without judgment or alteration.

Mastery Point Two
Detached Focus

Stress, fear and pain do not have a place when you function at your best. There is only a sense of accomplishment. To achieve this, you need to develop a special kind of awareness that allows you to open your perceptions to new options in thinking, feeling and movement. The special awareness is called Detached Focus. It helps you move with a sense of balance and great ease. You will be more relaxed, coordinated, integrated, and less susceptible to injuries. You will also be more open minded to new challenges and be able to expand your creativity. In the Detached Focus mode, your brain senses each body system respectively in a period of less than a split second and initiates action in a perfectly integrated way, thus your mind can express itself more efficiently through your body in motion. Your mind can also transcend obstacles in perception and see beyond what is seen.

Mastery Point Three
Shape Your Habits

There is no doubt that how you move is how you function. If the ultimate goal of martial arts training is the attainment of freedom, you cannot be free until you have entirely eliminated the obstacles that hinder your action. The more you accumulate things in your system, the heavier you become. The more habits you have, the less your body will be free. So losing habitual patterns that limit your movement and thinking is of primary importance to attaining your goals. It is an educational process that helps you get to know yourself and expand your full potential.

In that respect, learning new techniques should not be another process of piling up the size of your knowledge, but rather a streamlining process to filter what works for you from what others have done. Learning should be a process that gives your body a chance to go from receiving knowledge passively to exercising it actively.

Establish a framework of training without too much restriction. Never stop exploring new possibilities of your movement potential or fixing the way you think, move, and express your thoughts. The experience of enrichment comes from taking the risk of exposing yourself to a certain degree of uncertainty. When you restrict your thoughts, you restrict your movement too. When you free your movement, you can also free your mind. Mental liveliness brings effortless movement.

Organize your training in the way you can fill in the missing pieces in your life. Explore the new possibilities of what you have already known. Break down every movement into small segments so that your nervous system can examine and assimilate the unfamiliar territory, and eventually synthesize them into functional patterns of your own creation.

Gain fluidity in your performance by readjusting the way you move, think and feel. Try to move from within your body rather than from an effort to shape your external appearance. You can accomplish this by moving at your own pace without internal tension caused by pushing yourself to excel over others. Simply put, just be yourself. Explore who you are all about.

Mastery Point Four

Re-Pattern Your Habits

Be consciously aware of what is happening in your body when you move. Abandon your preconceived notions of technique and movement. Forget what you learned or what you think you should be doing.

Instead of doing purposeful, habitual movements, let the action happen. This helps you be able to perceive where movement comes from inside of you and what it reveals about yourself. You can sense the unconscious impulses and see the internal images of your movements when you break through the barrier of "should" and "have to" into the freedom to express your natural movement tendencies.

Mastery Point Five
Visualize Your Actions

In order to improve your techniques, you have to change the way you see things. The nervous system directs and coordinates all movement patterns, muscle use, and skeletal movement. Unbalanced muscle use can cause soft tissue and joint injuries. It also limits the range and vocabulary of your techniques.

To test your perception of your movements, imagine that there are lines of movement traveling through your body while you assume a relaxed standing position. Bring your weight to your left leg and then to your right leg. Squat lower and stand upright. Now move your body backward and forward. Each position reveals a specific location where you feel "right."

To find the most correct physical pattern for your body in more complex movements, use the following five areas of measurement to evaluate and correct your movement lines:

1) Align your skeletal positions and posture

Pay attention to all areas of your body and let go of excess tension in each part. Let your head float at the top of your spine while your shoulders drop and ease open to the sides. Let your ribs drop toward your feet and your back relax and stretch freely.

2) Balance your body and make a correct stance.

First begin with a static position to hold your posture properly for the activity you choose. Then balance yourself in continual dynamic movements as your weight constantly changes in space.

3) Achieve autonomy of body parts in movement.

Once you have aligned your posture and balanced your body, you can relax yourself into a deeper level of consciousness. Be aware of tension patterns in your movement and eliminate them. By cultivating awareness of yourself, you can discover how liberating it is to live as a vital, creative, moving being.

4) Move economically.

5) Release your energy.

Releasing is opening, emptying, playing, falling, jumping, spinning,. rising, and waiting. Releasing is letting your old energy go and new energy in. Releasing reduces tension.

Each movement has its own best directional pathway. By visualizing a particular process of movement, you initiate impulses along specific neural channels to particular muscles. Through a combination of practice and visualization, you can condition your nervous system to stimulate targeted muscles to respond for the intended movement.

Visualization is an effective method to maintain balanced alignment of the body's structure and therefore enhance your ability to perform precisely. It is your inner ability to see things that are not visually concrete, but do exist and affect your being. The more you visualize, the more efficient you become in the usage of your body.

Mastery Point Six
Inside Out

The cliché "action speaks louder than words" is true in martial arts. The way you appear often reveals much about your personality. Your body is a physical expression of your inner self. The way you move may reveals your dominant personality traits.

Recognize elements in your movement patterns that reflect things about you. Be aware of the unique way you do things. Discover what type of techniques are your favorite and where your movements originate from.

What angle do you take when you do certain techniques? Are you delicate or energetic in your performance? Explore the basic principles of movement structures and their purpose. Then let the movement happen and be self-directed. Do not impose yourself on the techniques or be imposed upon by them. There is no ideal movement or preconceived way to move. Be free to be yourself.

Mastery Point Seven
Check Your Movement Patterns

Through careful observation of your movement and inner feeling, you can find without difficulty that every movement has unique distinctions and patterns of its own no matter how simple it may be. The distinctive qualities are time, space, mass, and flow. Time is expressed abruptly or gradually. Space is the pathway through which your body moves. It is expressed directly or indirectly. Mass is your body weight which can be strong or light. Flow can be expressed as free movement or limited movement. Every movement has a different degree of all four elements.

You can also break down your movement into predictable patterns, for example: how you manifest your intentions, how you shift your weight, how you initiate a movement, your degree of spatial awareness, the smoothness of your movement, the rhythm of your breathing, your coordination, and your level of precision. Observation is a good method of reeducating your body. It helps you improve not only physical alignment, but also the efficiency, ease, and expressiveness of your body. You will experience more efficiency in the use of your deeper muscle groups through which you can have more range of motion and depth in your performance.

When you understand and incorporate these elements and patterns in your movement, you can perform in a relaxed way, feeling your entire body move in unison without breaking the fluid rhythm of your performance.

Mastery Point Eight
Understand Movement Types

Movement types generally fall into five categories. Use these categories to analyze and improve the patterns of movement in your martial arts practice.

1) Extending

Extending movement tends to be asymmetrical with sharp, straight lines, often diagonal angles arranged in a pushing motion. This is the most common movement in martial arts. Extending movements, particularly thrusting motions, manifest assertive power, focus, release, and reflexive patterns. Exhaling during extending movements adds power to the movement.

2) Contracting

Contracting is present in pulling activities. Free weight training and grappling techniques are good examples of contraction. Contracting movements involve the process of shortening the muscles, thus improving strength. Inhaling during contracting motions adds power to the movement.

3) Balancing

Generally speaking, every movement you do on one side of your body involves the other side as well. If you move your left arm or left leg, the opposite side responds. The same is true with forward and backward motions and the use of the upper and lower body. Balancing is the dominant movement pattern in walking, running, kicking, footwork, weaving, and throwing. It releases tension in the muscles and loosens the joints. Without balancing actions in your movements, your techniques will become stiff and awkward, take more energy to go from movement to movement and disturb the rhythm of your motion.

4) Shaping

Every movement has a shape. A technique you do with one side of your body always has a direct relationship with the other. It creates a holistic movement pattern. It has a distinctive effect of making a unique shape, good or bad. It shifts and places your weight when you move horizontally or vertically. It forms your posture and alignment. Shaping includes the height, width, angle, and alignment of your body parts. Having a good shape means your body has good alignment, spinal support, flexibility, and full movement potential and range. When you have poor shape in your movement, you experience misalignment and injury. The basic movements, kata, poomse, and hyung of martial arts are good examples of shaping systems.

5) Falling

Falling is an evasive movement. It has a direct connection with gravity and leverage. Be like liquid when you fall. By releasing the tension of your muscles and relaxing your mind, you can transform yourself into a soft being so that your body can absorb the shock of gravity.

Mastery Point Nine
Economize Your Action

For every martial artist it is vital to attain and maintain a uniformly developed body with a sound mind that is fully capable of naturally and easily performing varied tasks with spontaneous passion. In order to attain this quality you should analyze your movement patterns and identify any functional or structural problems. The problem areas should be kinesthetically redesigned to fit your needs.

Kinesthetic economy is achieved through developing balanced use of the muscles for ease of movement. The fundamental guideline is to change the movement in the way you can move from a stable and central core without strenuous effort. Every movement has three primary control centers: your torso, arms and legs. Watch your movement in the mirror and see what part of your body controls your movement during each segment of the performance. The position of your pelvis always plays a very important role in practicing techniques. Begin your analysis by concentrating on maintaining your pelvis in a neutral position so that your major muscle groups can support the spine and stabilize the torso.

You can also economize your movement by increasing your range of motion, correcting the misalignment of body parts, adjusting your weight distribution, and controlling your expenditure of energy. It is pointless to repeat a technique mindlessly hundreds of times. It is more beneficial to execute it only five to ten times slowly, mindfully, and patiently with rhythm and smoothness. For every technique, always try to execute specific placement of your body concentrating on correct execution, precise rhythm, and proper breath control. This is a good way to develop a clear awareness of which muscles enable you to move in a totally balanced and integrated way. The correct usage of your body and mind will eventually enable you to move your entire body as a single, integrated unit.

Mastery Point Ten
Body-Mind Connection

The human body is an assembly of masses (body parts). While you are resting or exercising, you need to align these masses properly to minimize the strain on any particular muscle group. Each mass has its respective weight (the exact proportion varies according to each individual). For example, the trunk takes approximately 44% of the whole body weight, each thigh and hip 10%, the head 6%, a shin 5%, an upper arm 4%, a forearm 3%, a foot 2%, and a hand 1%.

During your daily activities, your brain automatically chooses the easiest and most effective way to synchronize each mass so the whole body moves in unison. When you do any form of systematized exercise, you have to provide proper input for your brain to evaluate and synchronize each movement, since a new physical experience presents your brain with new information. In the process of learning, your brain breaks down movement patterns into functional segments to establish connections between the motor cortex of the brain and the muscle system.

Without improved changes in the brain and nervous system, it is not possible to have improvements in movement. In turn, the more completely you use the muscle system, the more you can increase brain activity which activates thinking and feeling. When these processes take place, you begin to experience fuller breathing, enhanced mental alertness, increased energy, better flexibility, increased range of motion, less headaches and back aches, better digestion, elevated mood, and enhanced sleep.

During the early stages of learning new skills, avoid difficult movements. If necessary, break down complex movements into easy segments. Try to make the easy movements enjoyable to perform rather than like work. When the movement is easy and pleasant to do, you don't have to force yourself to do it. It will become a part of your life. It is important to teach your brain without tiring the muscles. Let the naturalness of your movement take its course to help your brain discover what is right for your body so that your brain can help your body act with progressively enhanced efficiency. When your brain knows what your body is doing, your brain can choose the way in which your body can do it best.

Although you practice a form of martial arts developed by someone else, you should find your own ways of moving without forcing yourself to imitate your instructor or comparing yourself to others. You should make your own discovery of what is right for you. More than forty years of life experience have already provided you with enough information to make your own decisions about what works best for you. Keep things simple and in perspective. Be realistic. Find every possible way to establish a more complete self image. Constantly improve how you function. Listen to your body. Let your brain and body work together with minimal conscious interruptions.

Mastery Point Eleven
Raise Your Energy Level

Energy is the capacity to work. It is the source of power that generates our life force. It is the quality that distinguishes the animated from the inanimate. To die is to be a body without energy.

There are two types of energy: the visible and the invisible. Visible energy is what moves through the body and can be tracked, such as blood flow and nerve impulses. Invisible energy also moves through the body, but its structure and its functionality are not visible or measurable by untrained minds.

Exercise elevates the level of both visible and invisible energy. Visible energy is tangible and you know when you have it. Invisible energy is abstract and it needs to be explained for practical application to your practice.

The origin of invisible energy is from the philosophy of Taoism. According to Taoism, the universe is created from the Big Void, a formless, invisible being made of invisible energy. Everything in the universe arises from this energy and returns to it once its life is done. This original unity has no distinction of time and space. When this primary unity splits into two separate but complementary elements, they are called Yin and Yang.

Yin and Yang are opposing forces, working against each other and yet each containing its opposite. Each of these two forces is always in the process of becoming the other in a constant ebb and flow, contraction and expansion. This ever-changing relationship between the opposing forces influences all natural events. Each force controls, balances, and harmonizes the other. When balance is achieved between the two forces, health is attained. When there is disharmony between them, disease sprouts. So the attainment of balance is the objective, in this belief, to raise the energy level. Balance means the unimpeded flow of energy. When the balance of your physical, emotional and mental elements is blocked, you become agitated and dispirited.

The management of internal energy means you must let the opposite reside with you. Accept that you cannot solve every problem in your life but you can change your attitude in order to manage them without losing the true quality of your worth.

Mastery Point Twelve
Spontaneity Training

Attainment of the freedom of movement is one of the most important reasons of training in any sport or martial art. The freedom of movement means that you have sensitivity to your movement from the subtlest breath to your interactions with others. Spontaneity comes when you become free from the conscious hindrance of the body and the physical forces that govern movement: gravity, momentum and inertia. So the first step is to let go of fixed movement and move spontaneously, from an inner impulse, in accord with what your body is intrinsically capable of. There are billions of micro-movements within our body that we can't monitor externally. Deep within us we are always moving, even when we are asleep.

You can practice spontaneity training with a partner. For best results, keep in your mind the following two primary factors: sense yourself as a flowing presence and improvise your movement as you go along. You must stay focused not only on your action but also on your partner's. Perceive movement in your body that is working with or against gravity, momentum and inertia. Sense the inner feeling of your movement and reshape your movement based upon this feedback to fit in the relationship with your partner in space.

Try punching, kicking, and grappling. Use momentum to move in harmony with your partner rather than exert force to control him or her. Keep moving, irregularly changing the distance and points of contact between you and your partner.

Spontaneity training often leads you to see and feel yourself physically, emotionally and spiritually. It lessens your inhibitions about your performance in relation to others, which consequently helps you establish a sense of connectedness to others. It also reduces fear in physical contact situations. It's fun. It makes you playful and creative. Since it requires a sense of balance and unexpectedness, it often stimulates unused brain functions.

Through spontaneity training you may become aware of your personality traits. You may discover what type of person you are: an initiator or follower, risk taker or passive receiver. It is a self-education of how to give in to your strength and to maximize the effectiveness of your movement without risking your safety. You can enliven yourself from the inside out, which will result in a greater dynamic expression of your biological potential.

As you progress, you may create more unpredictable movements in varied rhythms. Scientists say that they are much more stimulating to the brain than predictable movement patterns. When you attain spontaneity in your movement, you can shake yourself out of the rigidity and dive deeply into the endless possibility of your physical movement.

ABOUT THE AUTHOR

Sang H. Kim is an internationally acclaimed authority on martial arts, author of seven martial arts books and star of over forty instructional video tapes. Dr. Kim travels extensively throughout the world presenting martial arts seminars and motivational lectures. He continues to actively pursue his martial arts training, holding master rankings in taekwondo, hapkido, junsado and kumdo.

INDEX